The Essential Herbert

George Herbert

BORN 3 APRIL 1593
DIED 3 MARCH 1633

The Essential HERBERT

Selected and with an
Introduction by

ANTHONY HECHT

The Ecco Press
New York

Published in 1987 by The Ecco Press
26 West 17th Street, New York, N.Y. 10011
Published simultaneously in Canada by
Penguin Books Canada Ltd., Ontario
Printed in the United States of America
Designed by Reg Perry

Library of Congress Cataloging in Publication Data
Herbert, George, 1593-1633.
The essential Herbert.
(The Essential poets; v. 5)
I. Hecht, Anthony, 1923- . II. Title.
III. Series: Essential poets (New York, N.Y.); v. 5.
PR3507.A4 1987 821'.3 87-6744
ISBN 0-88001-158-0
ISBN 0-88001-159-9 (pbk.)

Engraving of Herbert by R. White first appeared
in Izaak Walton's Life, *1670*

Contents

To Hays and Linda Rockwell

Lovely enchanting language, sugar-cane,
Hony of roses, whither wilt thou flie?

Introduction

I don't know who it was that came up with the term "confessional poets" to embrace a crew as distinct from one another as Robert Lowell, W. D. Snodgrass, Sylvia Plath, Anne Sexton and Allen Ginsberg, but whatever convenience the label may confer is paid for at the obvious cost of accuracy, for it applies more justly to George Herbert than to any modern poet. In his little handbook of the pastoral vocation, *The Country Parson,* Herbert writes of the priest that ". . . in his visiting the sick, or otherwise afflicted, he followeth the Churches counsell, namely, in persuading them to particular confession, labouring to make them understand the great good use of this antient and pious ordinance. . . ." And Herbert's great book of poems, *The Temple,* is precisely confessional in double senses of the word: an acknowledgment of his faults and weaknesses, and also a declaration or avowal of faith. See, for example, "The Reprisall."

Of course, Herbert has also been bracketed under the label of "metaphysical poets" with, among others, Donne and Marvell, and we are no less conscious of his clear difference from both of them. Donne is a special favorite of modern readers, and not least of all for the frank and good-humored eroticism of his secular poetry, as well as the rather shocking way he blends religious and erotic elements in both love and devotional poems, a liberty for which his final religious poems are sometimes seen as a late and fevered apology. Marvell's concern with sex is more discreet (or covert, if you prefer) but it should also be added that for him a religious stance was virtually the equivalent of a political one, and even his most religious poems are resolutely secular. Both Donne and Marvell brilliantly employed the vein of satire, exhibiting malice and comedy with delighted glee. But Herbert rejected these modes, or, more accurately, never entertained the notion of employing them.

The "metaphysical" label, going back to Dr. Johnson's essay on Cowley, and perhaps beyond that to Dryden's comment that Donne "affects the metaphysics, not only in his satires, but in his amorous verses, where nature only should reign; and perplexes the minds of the fair sex with nice speculations of philosophy, when he should engage their hearts, and entertain them with the softnesses of love . . . ," was given fresh currency by Herbert Grierson's famous anthology, and still more so by T. S. Eliot's review of it, his celebrated essay "The Metaphysical Poets" (1921), which effectively changed the course of poetic taste in our time. And beyond question there are plain resemblances, sometimes outright borrowings, that link Herbert to Donne, and Vaughan and Crashaw to Herbert. That poets should admire and imitate one another is nothing strange; Dryden observed of Ben Jonson, "He invades Authors like a Monarch, and what would be theft in other Poets, is onely victory in him."

There will be a brand of reader determined to reject Herbert, and perhaps all religious poetry, maintaining with Marx that religion is the "opium of the people." But no one can read through the poems presented here and come away still holding that view. First of all, Herbert's poetry founds itself on an incomparable intimacy, and an urgency in his relations with God so intense that, in the words of Douglas Bush, "with all his sophisticated art, he seems unaware of his audience, so that we rather overhear him than read him." Then, as Eliot has thoughtfully observed, "The great danger for the poet who would write religious verse, is that of setting down what he would like to feel rather than be faithful to the expression of what he really feels. Of such pious insincerity Herbert is never guilty." And these poems offer us instances of not only matchless serenity, joy or gratitude, but in equal measure frustration, anger, insubordination, deprivation and grief. The religious life is by no means easier than the secular life, whatever the skeptics may suppose, and for Herbert it was in a number of important ways more difficult. He had intended a quite different one, probably as a diplomat (he was at ease in at least six languages: French, Spanish, Italian, Latin, Greek and English), possibly as a secretary of state. And when quite suddenly his worldly hopes failed with the deaths of two influential friends, followed by the death of King James I, who had greatly admired him, and when his remarkable mother, as well perhaps as Bishop Lancelot Andrewes, had urged him toward a religious vocation, he came to it at length by way of agonizing vacillations, regrets and uncertainties. All these equivocations he records in his poems, which are personal versions of the full range of the psalms, hymns and lauds of the liturgy, from the cry of the Twenty-second Psalm, "My God, my God, why hast thou forsaken me," which is also the cry from the Cross, to the Gloria in Excelsis.

Like others of his time and faith, he found himself caught between the Scylla and Charybdis of antinomian, self-accrediting Puritans and non-Conformists on the one hand, and on the other what many of his contemporaries saw as the corrupted and corrupting tyranny and misappropriated authority of the Church of Rome, to them Revelation's whore of Babylon. But in contrast to such embattled attitudes Herbert, in the words of Bush, "deplored the worm of schism eating away at the English rose," and rarely (once in Latin, once in English) exhibited any view of another Christian sect in an unfavorable light. Bush adds, "It is to Herbert's writings and life that we owe much of our picture of the order, strength, and beauty of seventeenth-century Anglicanism at its best."

The drama of Herbert's life was largely inward. This is the sort of drama about which Flaubert wrote to Louise Colet, "I maintain that ideas are events. It is more difficult to make them interesting, I know, but if you fail the style is at fault." It is also what Hannah Arendt has in mind when in the volume *Thinking* in *The Life of the Mind,* she writes of thinkers (a term which could embrace all contemplatives, and many poets), "Were we to follow Greek linguistic custom, by which the 'heroes,' acting men in the highest sense, were called *andres epiphaneis,* men who are fully manifest, highly conspicuous, then we would call thinkers the inconspicuous men by definition and profession." The main *facts* of Herbert's life are briefly and beautifully recounted by Izaak Walton in a biography that some (I am not one of these) find too reverent. It was Herbert's happy and successful career at Cambridge, together with his acquaintance with the great and the powerful (including, besides the king, Sir Francis Bacon, whom Walton calls "the great Secretary of Nature") that encouraged his hopes for a worldly career. When these were disappointed he did not attain clerical celebrity, as did John Donne, who was the most famous preacher of his day, and dean of St. Paul's. In the last three or so years of his life Herbert married very happily, took holy orders and duties in the obscure country parish of Bemerton, and wrote most of the poems by which he is remembered.

Eliot's essay on the metaphysical poets contains his celebrated and much debated phrase on the "dissociation of sensibility." He declares, "Tennyson and Browning are poets, and they think; but they do not feel their thoughts as immediately as the odour of a rose. A thought to Donne was an experience; it modified his sensibility." A lot of wasteful comment has clustered around this almost mystic formulation about the capacity to "feel a thought," the symbolism of the rose and its perfume. But Eliot continues more precisely: "In the seventeenth century a dissociation of sensibility set in, from which we have never recovered; and this dissociation, as is natural, was aggravated by the influence of the two most powerful poets of the century, Milton and Dryden. . . . The sentimental age began early in the eighteenth century, and continued. The poets revolted against the ratiocinative . . . they thought and felt by fits."

It seems to me that Dryden's strictures on Donne's "amorous verses" bears out Eliot's point exactly. In Dryden's view, love poems should not be witty, nor should they tax unduly the mental abilities of the ladies they are supposed to please, or to seduce. Apart from the slur on the intelligence of women, there is the "sentimental" assumption that love is a soft, mushy, inward turbulence, where the ratiocinative faculties, wit, mental agility, learning and complexity of thought must have no place. But the delight of such seduction poems as "To His Coy Mistress" or "The Extasie" resides in large part to their brilliant ingenuity; they are as *cunning* as Marlowe's Leander, that "bold sharp sophister" who, like a university debater, "demonstrates" that chastity (a) is not a virtue, and (b) doesn't exist; or as captivating as the witty, romantic banter of such Shakespearean heroines as Rosalind or Beatrice. Their intricate combination of passion, levity and intelligence commends them, and we have learned to applaud the marriage of love and wit.

We are less prepared, however, to applaud the marriage of wit and piety. In a nation whose airwaves quiver with the images and vibrato admonitions of millionaire evangelists, it is common to suppose that divine worship is a largely visceral and rhythmic experience; and fundamentalism in certain specific ways is a doctrine that excludes rather than encourages thought. Though we find we can tolerate, and even enjoy, the surprising and unexpected sentiment of Donne's

> *I can love any, so she be not true*

with its cynical mockery of fidelity, its unembarrassed declaration for freedom and promiscuity, or his

> *If thou love me, take heed of loving me*

with its "verbal" paradox, we are probably more astonished by Herbert's

Ah my deare God! though I am clean forgot,
Let me not love thee, if I love thee not.

And yet what Herbert has done is wittily to appropriate the conventions of love poetry. "A Parodie" converts a secular love poem, probably by the Earl of Pembroke, to pious usage, and "Jordan [1]" is full of allusions to the Petrarchan conventions.

His poems exhibit a very wide range of ingenuity and improvisation. There are hidden acrostics, emblematic forms, anagrams, puns and considerable learning. There is such abundance here that, as Joseph Summers says, "The poems . . . will repay almost any amount of study we may wish to devote to them." And of course scholarly and critical studies abound. These would begin with the fine Oxford edition, edited by F. E. Hutchinson, with its full apparatus, notes and commentaries. They would also include Rosemond Tuve's *A Reading of George Herbert,* Joseph Summers's *George Herbert: His Religion & Art,* Arnold Stein's *George Herbert's Lyrics,* along with a very large number of essays and briefer comments.

No doubt such commentary can aid a reader considerably, because for all the simplicity of Herbert's language his poems are by no means simple. They require, among other things, a familiarity with Scripture, a good dictionary and a willingness to consider words and ideas long and carefully. But we would cheat ourselves of a major pleasure this poetry affords if we were to treat it as a sort of puzzle or set of riddles for which Professor X has provided all the answers in his book, and to whom we can turn to relieve ourselves of the burden of serious thought. "We must enjoy the poetry before we attempt to penetrate the poet's mind; we must enjoy it before we understand it, if the attempt to understand is to be worth the trouble," writes Eliot. "We begin by enjoying poems, and lines in poems, which make an immediate impression; only gradually, as we familiarise ourselves with the whole work, do we appreciate *The Temple* as a coherent sequence of poems. . . ."

And this selection is addressed to such enterprising readers. Among the incidental felicities and ingenuities that may first strike and delight them, there are two that deserve at least brief mention, and they are related. One is Herbert's formal inventiveness. Even his sonnets are innovative: "Prayer [1]" is not a sentence, having no main verb, yet it is still a sonnet, observing the formal rules of rhyme and meter, as do Herbert's several sonnets. But this is almost the only standard form he employs. Each of his poems other than the sonnets seems to find, discover or invent its own form, and these forms tend often to be unusually demanding. Perhaps the nearest Herbert comes to formal freedom appears in that poem of metrical and emotional rebellion, "The Collar." The formal originality and individuality of these poems seem to emphasize the freshness, uniqueness and novelty of each spiritual experience the poet presents, to enhance the excitement of unprecedentedness that belongs to any new experience. The forms themselves are witty, exacting from the poet elaborate pains and planning; but they are also an index of the care he takes in his dealings with his God.

The second sort of pleasure concerns Herbert's fascination with music. He was himself a skillful musician, a lutanist and a composer who may have set some of his own texts, perhaps "A Dialogue-Antheme," for example. In his poems he uses musical metaphors, consonance and dissonance, and even musical forms themselves: for example, "Sinnes round" is a serious adaptation of the usually convivial canon or round, sung in parts, and essentially circular and repetitious. Music is also a factor of stanzaic patterns, of rhymes, echoes, refrains, and of the whole pastoral tradition in which all shepherds and pastors, following King David, as well as Virgil's and Spenser's spokesmen, are singers first and last. The diction of this poetry is of an unsurpassed purity, a triumph of *style* that, according to Flaubert, could animate ideas and turn them into events. And the events of Herbert's life are chiefly those of the spirit.

One of the most moving and eloquent of details in Walton's *Life* concerns Herbert's deathbed directions for the disposition of his poems. He had them sent to his friend Nicholas Ferrar, head of the Anglican community at Little Gidding, with these words of instruction to his messenger and close attendant, Mr. Duncon:

> *Sir, I pray deliver this little Book to my dear brother Ferrar, and tell him, he shall find in it a picture of the many spiritual Conflicts that have passed betwixt God and my Soul, before I could subject mine to the will of* Jesus my Master: *in whose service I have now found perfect freedom; desire him to read it: and then, if he can think it may turn to the advantage of any dejected poor Soul, let it be made publick: if not, let him burn it: for* I and it, are less than the least of God's mercies.

Ferrar was not a poet, but he saw the merit of this work, and salvaged it from what would have been the ashes of oblivion. As such, it stands as a monument with at least two other great works of art preserved to us by a happy fate: the *Aeneid,* with which Virgil was dissatisfied and which he wanted to have destroyed, but which was saved at the bidding of the Emperor Augustus; and the sole cast equestrian statue to survive from antiquity, the mounted figure of Marcus Aurelius that has for years adorned the Capitoline Hill in Rome, exempted from being melted down for the use of its metal because it was mistakenly thought to be the Christian emperor Constantine.

If this book finds its way into the hands of some grateful readers who had never met with Herbert's work before, it will achieve everything its editor can hope for it. Introducing me to the works of certain poets has been one of the greatest services that a few other poets, teachers and friends have done me, and I should be proud to have done as much for others, and not least for total strangers.

—ANTHONY HECHT

The Essential Herbert

Poems

THE CHURCH

The Altar

A broken Altar, Lord, thy servant reares,
Made of a heart, and cemented with teares:
Whose parts are as thy hand did frame;
No workmans tool hath touch'd the same.
A HEART alone
Is such a stone,
As nothing but
Thy pow'r doth cut.
Wherefore each part
Of my hard heart
Meets in this frame,
To praise thy Name:
That, if I chance to hold my peace,
These stones to praise thee may not cease.
O let thy blessed SACRIFICE be mine,
And sanctifie this ALTAR to be thine.

The Sacrifice

Oh all ye, who passe by, whose eyes and minde
To worldly things are sharp, but to me blinde;
To me, who took eyes that I might you finde:
Was ever grief like mine?

The Princes of my people make a head
Against their Maker: they do wish me dead,
Who cannot wish, except I give them bread:
Was ever grief like mine?

Without me each one, who doth now me brave,
Had to this day been an Egyptian slave.
They use that power against me, which I gave:
Was ever grief like mine?

Mine own Apostle, who the bag did beare,
Though he had all I had, did not forbeare
To sell me also, and to put me there:
Was ever grief like mine?

For thirtie pence he did my death devise,
Who at three hundred did the ointment prize,
Not half so sweet as my sweet sacrifice:
Was ever grief like mine?

Therefore my soul melts, and my hearts deare treasure
Drops bloud (the onely beads) my words to measure:
O let this cup passe, if it be thy pleasure:
Was ever grief like mine?

These drops being temper'd with a sinners tears
A Balsome are for both the Hemispheres:
Curing all wounds, but mine; all, but my fears:
Was ever grief like mine?

Yet my Disciples sleep: I cannot gain
One houre of watching; but their drowsie brain
Comforts not me, and doth my doctrine stain:
Was ever grief like mine?

Arise, arise, they come. Look how they runne!
Alas! what haste they make to be undone!
How with their lanterns do they seek the sunne!
Was ever grief like mine?

With clubs and staves they seek me, as a thief,
Who am the Way and Truth, the true relief;
Most true to those, who are my greatest grief:
Was ever grief like mine?

Judas, dost thou betray me with a kisse?
Canst thou finde hell about my lips? and misse
Of life, just at the gates of life and blisse?
Was ever grief like mine?

See, they lay hold on me, not with the hands
Of faith, but furie: yet at their commands
I suffer binding, who have loos'd their bands:
Was ever grief like mine?

All my Disciples flie; fear puts a barre
Betwixt my friends and me. They leave the starre,
That brought the wise men of the East from farre.
Was ever grief like mine?

Then from one ruler to another bound
They leade me; urging, that it was not sound
What I taught: Comments would the text confound.
Was ever grief like mine?

The Priest and rulers all false witness seek
'Gainst him, who seeks not life, but is the meek
And readie Paschal Lambe of this great week:
Was ever grief like mine?

Then they accuse me of great blasphemie,
That I did thrust into the Deitie,
Who never thought that any robberie:
Was ever grief like mine?

Some said, that I the Temple to the floore
In three dayes raz'd, and raised as before.
Why, he that built the world can do much more:
Was ever grief like mine?

Then they condemne me all with that same breath,
Which I do give them daily, unto death.
Thus *Adam* my first breathing rendereth:
Was ever grief like mine?

They binde, and leade me unto *Herod:* he
Sends me to *Pilate.* This makes them agree;
But yet their friendship is my enmitie:
Was ever grief like mine?

Herod and all his bands do set me light,
Who teach all hands to warre, fingers to fight,
And onely am the Lord of Hosts and might:
Was ever grief like mine?

Herod in judgement sits, while I do stand;
Examines me with a censorious hand:
I him obey, who all things else command:
Was ever grief like mine?

The *Jews* accuse me with despitefulnesse;
And vying malice with my gentlenesse,
Pick quarrels with their onely happinesse:
Was ever grief like mine?

I answer nothing, but with patience prove
If stonie hearts will melt with gentle love.
But who does hawk at eagles with a dove?
Was ever grief like mine?

My silence rather doth augment their crie;
My dove doth back into my bosome flie,
Because the raging waters still are high:
Was ever grief like mine?

Heark how they crie aloud still, *Crucifie:*
It is not fit he live a day, they crie,
Who cannot live lesse then eternally:
Was ever grief like mine?

Pilate, a stranger, holdeth off; but they,
Mine owne deare people, cry, *Away, away,*
With noises confused frighting the day:
Was ever grief like mine?

Yet still they shout, and crie, and stop their eares,
Putting my life among their sinnes and fears,
And therefore wish *my bloud on them and theirs:*
Was ever grief like mine?

See how spite cankers things. These words aright
Used, and wished, are the whole worlds light:
But hony is their gall, brightnesse their night:
Was ever grief like mine?

They choose a murderer, and all agree
In him to do themselves a courtesie:
For it was their own case who killed me:
Was ever grief like mine?

And a seditious murderer he was:
But I the Prince of peace; peace that doth passe
All understanding, more then heav'n doth glasse:
Was ever grief like mine?

Why, Cæsar is their onely King, not I:
He clave the stonie rock, when they were drie;
But surely not their hearts, as I well trie:
Was ever grief like mine?

Ah! how they scourge me! yet my tendernesse
Doubles each lash: and yet their bitternesse
Windes up my grief to a mysteriousnesse:
Was ever grief like mine?

They buffet him, and box him as they list,
Who grasps the earth and heaven with his fist,
And never yet, whom he would punish, miss'd:
Was ever grief like mine?

Behold, they spit on me in scornfull wise,
Who by my spittle gave the blinde man eies,
Leaving his blindnesse to my enemies:
Was ever grief like mine?

My face they cover, though it be divine.
As *Moses* face was vailed, so is mine,
Lest on their double-dark souls either shine:
Was ever grief like mine?

Servants and abjects flout me; they are wittie:
Now prophesie who strikes thee, is their dittie.
So they in me denie themselves all pitie:
Was ever grief like mine?

And now I am deliver'd unto death,
Which each one calls for so with utmost breath,
That he before me well nigh suffereth:
Was ever grief like mine?

Weep not, deare friends, since I for both have wept
When all my tears were bloud, the while you slept:
Your tears for your own fortunes should be kept:
Was ever grief like mine?

The souldiers lead me to the Common Hall;
There they deride me, they abuse me all:
Yet for twelve heav'nly legions I could call:
Was ever grief like mine?

Then with a scarlet robe they me aray;
Which shews my bloud to be the onely way
And cordiall left to repair mans decay:
Was ever grief like mine?

Then on my head a crown of thorns I wear:
For these are all the grapes *Sion* doth bear,
Though I my vine planted and watred there:
Was ever grief like mine?

So sits the earths great curse in *Adams* fall
Upon my head: so I remove it all
From th' earth unto my brows, and bear the thrall:
Was ever grief like mine?

Then with the reed they gave to me before,
They strike my head, the rock from whence all store
Of heav'nly blessings issue evermore:
Was ever grief like mine?

They bow their knees to me, and cry, *Hail king:*
What ever scoffes & scornfulnesse can bring,
I am the floore, the sink, where they it fling:
Was ever grief like mine?

Yet since mans scepters are as frail as reeds,
And thorny all their crowns, bloudie their weeds;
I, who am Truth, turn into truth their deeds:
Was ever grief like mine?

The souldiers also spit upon that face,
Which Angels did desire to have the grace,
And Prophets, once to see, but found no place:
Was ever grief like mine?

Thus trimmed, forth they bring me to the rout,
Who *Crucifie him,* crie with one strong shout.
God holds his peace at man, and man cries out:
Was ever grief like mine?

They leade me in once more, and putting then
Mine own clothes on, they leade me out agen.
Whom devils flie, thus is he toss'd of men:
Was ever grief like mine?

And now wearie of sport, glad to ingrosse
All spite in one, counting my life their losse,
They carrie me to my most bitter crosse:
Was ever grief like mine?

My crosse I bear my self, untill I faint:
Then Simon bears it for me by constraint,
The decreed burden of each mortall Saint:
Was ever grief like mine?

O all ye who passe by, behold and see;
Man stole the fruit, but I must climbe the tree;
The tree of life to all, but onely me:
Was ever grief like mine?

Lo, here I hang, charg'd with a world of sinne,
The greater world o' th' two; for that came in
By words, but this by sorrow I must win:
Was ever grief like mine?

Such sorrow as, if sinfull man could feel,
Or feel his part, he would not cease to kneel,
Till all were melted, though he were all steel:
Was ever grief like mine?

But, *O my God, my God!* why leav'st thou me,
The sonne, in whom thou dost delight to be?
My God, my God——
Never was grief like mine.

Shame tears my soul, my bodie many a wound;
Sharp nails pierce this, but sharper that confound;
Reproches, which are free, while I am bound.
Was ever grief like mine?

Now heal thy self, Physician; now come down.
Alas! I did so, when I left my crown
And fathers smile for you, to feel his frown:
Was ever grief like mine?

In healing not my self, there doth consist
All that salvation, which ye now resist;
Your safetie in my sicknesse doth subsist:
Was ever grief like mine?

Betwixt two theeves I spend my utmost breath,
As he that for some robberie suffereth.
Alas! what have I stollen from you? Death.
Was ever grief like mine?

A king my title is, prefixt on high;
Yet by my subjects am condemn'd to die
A servile death in servile companie:
Was ever grief like mine?

They give me vineger mingled with gall,
But more with malice: yet, when they did call,
With Manna, Angels food, I fed them all:
Was ever grief like mine?

They part my garments, and by lot dispose
My coat, the type of love, which once cur'd those
Who sought for help, never malicious foes:
Was ever grief like mine?

Nay, after death their spite shall further go;
For they will pierce my side, I full well know;
That as sinne came, so Sacraments might flow:
Was ever grief like mine?

But now I die; now all is finished.
My wo, mans weal: and now I bow my head.
Onely let others say, when I am dead,
Never was grief like mine.

The Thanksgiving

Oh King of grief! (a title strange, yet true,
To thee of all kings onely due)

Oh King of wounds! how shall I grieve for thee,
Who in all grief preventest me?
Shall I weep bloud? why, thou hast wept such store
That all thy body was one doore.
Shall I be scourged, flouted, boxed, sold?
'Tis but to tell the tale is told.
My God, my God, why dost thou part from me?
Was such a grief as cannot be.
Shall I then sing, skipping thy dolefull storie,
And side with thy triumphant glorie?
Shall thy strokes be my stroking? thorns, my flower?
Thy rod, my posie? crosse, my bower?
But how then shall I imitate thee, and
Copie thy fair, though bloudie hand?
Surely I will revenge me on thy love,
And trie who shall victorious prove.
If thou dost give me wealth, I will restore
All back unto thee by the poore.
If thou dost give me honour, men shall see,
The honour doth belong to thee.
I will not marry; or, if she be mine,
She and her children shall be thine.
My bosome friend, if he blaspheme thy Name,
I will tear thence his love and fame.
One half of me being gone, the rest I give
Unto some Chappell, die or live.
As for thy passion — But of that anon,
When with the other I have done.
For thy predestination I'le contrive,
That three yeares hence, if I survive,
I'le build a spittle, or mend common wayes,
But mend mine own without delayes.
Then I will use the works of thy creation,
As if I us'd them but for fashion.
The world and I will quarrell; and the yeare

Shall not perceive, that I am here.
My musick shall finde thee, and ev'ry string
Shall have his attribute to sing;
That all together may accord in thee,
And prove one God, one harmonie.
If thou shalt give me wit, it shall appeare,
If thou hast giv'n it me, 'tis here.
Nay, I will reade thy book, and never move
Till I have found therein thy love,
Thy art of love, which I'le turn back on thee:
O my deare Saviour, Victorie!
Then for thy passion — I will do for that —
Alas, my God, I know not what.

The Reprisall

I have consider'd it, and finde
There is no dealing with thy mighty passion:
For though I die for thee, I am behinde;
My sinnes deserve the condemnation.

O make me innocent, that I
May give a disentangled state and free:
And yet thy wounds still my attempts defie,
For by thy death I die for thee.

Ah! was it not enough that thou
By thy eternall glorie didst outgo me?
Couldst thou not griefs sad conquests me allow,
But in all vic'tries overthrow me?

Yet by confession will I come
Into thy conquest: though I can do nought

Against thee, in thee I will overcome
The man, who once against thee fought.

The Agonie

Philosophers have measur'd mountains,
Fathom'd the depths of seas, of states, and kings,
Walk'd with a staffe to heav'n, and traced fountains:
But there are two vast, spacious things,
The which to measure it doth more behove:
Yet few there are that sound them; Sinne and Love.

Who would know Sinne, let him repair
Unto Mount Olivet; there shall he see
A man so wrung with pains, that all his hair,
His skinne, his garments bloudie be.
Sinne is that presse and vice, which forceth pain
To hunt his cruell food through ev'ry vein.

Who knows not Love, let him assay
And taste that juice, which on the crosse a pike
Did set again abroach; then let him say
If ever he did taste the like.
Love is that liquor sweet and most divine,
Which my God feels as bloud; but I, as wine.

Redemption

Having been tenant long to a rich Lord,
Not thriving, I resolved to be bold,
And make a suit unto him, to afford
A new small-rented lease, and cancell th' old.

In heaven at his manour I him sought:
They told me there, that he was lately gone
About some land, which he had dearly bought
Long since on earth, to take possession.
I straight return'd, and knowing his great birth,
Sought him accordingly in great resorts;
In cities, theatres, gardens, parks, and courts:
At length I heard a ragged noise and mirth
Of theeves and murderers: there I him espied,
Who straight, *Your suit is granted,* said, & died.

Sepulchre

O Blessed bodie! Whither art thou thrown?
No lodging for thee, but a cold hard stone?
So many hearts on earth, and yet not one
Receive thee?

Sure there is room within our hearts good store;
For they can lodge transgressions by the score:
Thousands of toyes dwell there, yet out of doore
They leave thee.

But that which shews them large, shews them unfit.
What ever sinne did this pure rock commit,
Which holds thee now? Who hath indited it
Of murder?

Where our hard hearts have took up stones to brain thee,
And missing this, most falsly did arraigne thee;
Onely these stones in quiet entertain thee,
And order.

And as of old the Law by heav'nly art
Was writ in stone; so thou, which also art
The letter of the word, find'st no fit heart
To hold thee.

Yet do we still persist as we began,
And so should perish, but that nothing can,
Though it be cold, hard, foul, from loving man
Withhold thee.

Easter

Rise heart; thy Lord is risen. Sing his praise
Without delayes,
Who takes thee by the hand, that thou likewise
With him mayst rise:
That, as his death calcined thee to dust,
His life may make thee gold, and much more, just.

Awake, my lute, and struggle for thy part
With all thy art.
The crosse taught all wood to resound his name,
Who bore the same.
His stretched sinews taught all strings, what key
Is best to celebrate this most high day.

Consort both heart and lute, and twist a song
Pleasant and long:
Or, since all musick is but three parts vied
And multiplied,
O let thy blessed Spirit bear a part,
And make up our defects with his sweet art.

I got me flowers to straw thy way;
I got me boughs off many a tree:
But thou wast up by break of day,
And brought'st thy sweets along with thee.

The Sunne arising in the East,
Though he give light, & th' East perfume;
If they should offer to contest
With thy arising, they presume.

Can there be any day but this,
Though many sunnes to shine endeavour?
We count three hundred, but we misse:
There is but one, and that one ever.

Easter-wings

Lord, who createdst man in wealth and store,
Though foolishly he lost the same,
Decaying more and more,
Till he became
Most poore:
With thee
O let me rise
As larks, harmoniously,
And sing this day thy victories:
Then shall the fall further the flight in me.

My tender age in sorrow did beginne:
And still with sicknesses and shame
Thou didst so punish sinne,
That I became
Most thinne,

With thee
Let me combine
And feel this day thy victorie:
For, if I imp my wing on thine,
Affliction shall advance the flight in me.

H. Baptisme [II]

Since, Lord, to thee
A narrow way and little gate
Is all the passage, on my infancie
Thou didst lay hold, and antedate
My faith in me.

O let me still
Write thee great God, and me a childe:
Let me be soft and supple to thy will,
Small to my self, to others milde,
Behither ill.

Although by stealth
My flesh get on, yet let her sister
My soul bid nothing, but preserve her wealth:
The growth of flesh is but a blister;
Childhood is health.

Sinne [I]

Lord, with what care hast thou begirt us round!
Parents first season us: then schoolmasters
Deliver us to laws; they send us bound
To rules of reason, holy messengers,

Pulpits and Sundayes, sorrow dogging sinne,
Afflictions sorted, anguish of all sizes,
Fine nets and stratagems to catch us in,
Bibles laid open, millions of surprises,
Blessings beforehand, tyes of gratefulnesse,
The sound of glorie ringing in our eares:
Without, our shame; within, our consciences;
Angels and grace, eternall hopes and fears.
Yet all these fences and their whole aray
One cunning bosome-sinne blows quite away.

Affliction [1]

When first thou didst entice to thee my heart,
I thought the service brave:
So many joyes I writ down for my part,
Besides what I might have
Out of my stock of naturall delights,
Augmented with thy gracious benefits.

I looked on thy furniture so fine,
And made it fine to me:
Thy glorious houshold-stuffe did me entwine,
And 'tice me unto thee.
Such starres I counted mine: both heav'n and earth
Payd me my wages in a world of mirth.

What pleasures could I want, whose King I served,
Where joyes my fellows were?
Thus argu'd into hopes, my thoughts reserved
No place for grief or fear.
Therefore my sudden soul caught at the place,
And made her youth and fiercenesse seek thy face.

At first thou gav'st me milk and sweetnesses;
I had my wish and way:
My dayes were straw'd with flow'rs and happinesse;
There was no moneth but May.
But with my yeares sorrow did twist and grow,
And made a partie unawares for wo.

My flesh began unto my soul in pain,
Sicknesses cleave my bones;
Consuming agues dwell in ev'ry vein,
And tune my breath to grones.
Sorrow was all my soul; I scarce beleeved,
Till grief did tell me roundly, that I lived.

When I got health, thou took'st away my life,
And more; for my friends die:
My mirth and edge was lost; a blunted knife
Was of more use then I.
Thus thinne and lean without a fence or friend,
I was blown through with ev'ry storm and winde.

Whereas my birth and spirit rather took
The way that takes the town;
Thou didst betray me to a lingring book,
And wrap me in a gown.
I was entangled in the world of strife,
Before I had the power to change my life.

Yet, for I threatned oft the siege to raise,
Not simpring all mine age,
Thou often didst with Academick praise
Melt and dissolve my rage.
I took thy sweetned pill, till I came where
I could not go away, nor persevere.

Yet lest perchance I should too happie be
In my unhappinesse,
Turning my purge to food, thou throwest me
Into more sicknesses.
Thus doth thy power crosse-bias me, not making
Thine own gift good, yet me from my wayes taking.

Now I am here, what thou wilt do with me
None of my books will show:
I reade, and sigh, and wish I were a tree;
For sure then I would grow
To fruit or shade: at least some bird would trust
Her houshold to me, and I should be just.

Yet, though thou troublest me, I must be meek;
In weaknesse must be stout.
Well, I will change the service, and go seek
Some other master out.
Ah my deare God! though I am clean forgot,
Let me not love thee, if I love thee not.

Repentance

Lord, I confesse my sinne is great;
Great is my sinne. Oh! gently treat
With thy quick flow'r, thy momentarie bloom;
Whose life still pressing
Is one undressing,
A steadie aiming at a tombe.

Mans age is two houres work, or three:
Each day doth round about us see.

Thus are we to delights: but we are all
To sorrows old,
If life be told
From what life feeleth, Adams fall.

O let thy height of mercie then
Compassionate short-breathed men.
Cut me not off for my most foul transgression:
I do confesse
My foolishnesse;
My God, accept of my confession.

Sweeten at length this bitter bowl,
Which thou hast pour'd into my soul;
Thy wormwood turn to health, windes to fair weather:
For if thou stay,
I and this day,
As we did rise, we die together.

When thou for sinne rebukest man,
Forthwith he waxeth wo and wan:
Bitternesse fills our bowels; all our hearts
Pine, and decay,
And drop away,
And carrie with them th' other parts.

But thou wilt sinne and grief destroy;
That so the broken bones may joy,
And tune together in a well-set song,
Full of his praises,
Who dead men raises.
Fractures well cur'd make us more strong.

Faith

Lord, how couldst thou so much appease
Thy wrath for sinne as, when mans sight was dimme,
And could see little, to regard his ease,
And bring by Faith all things to him?

Hungrie I was, and had no meat:
I did conceit a most delicious feast;
I had it straight, and did as truly eat,
As ever did a welcome guest.

There is a rare outlandish root,
Which when I could not get, I thought it here:
That apprehension cur'd so well my foot,
That I can walk to heav'n well neare.

I owed thousands and much more:
I did beleeve that I did nothing owe,
And liv'd accordingly; my creditor
Beleeves so too, and lets me go.

Faith makes me any thing, or all
That I beleeve is in the sacred storie:
And where sinne placeth me in Adams fall,
Faith sets me higher in his glorie.

If I go lower in the book,
What can be lower then the common manger?
Faith puts me there with him, who sweetly took
Our flesh and frailtie, death and danger.

If blisse had lien in art or strength,
None but the wise or strong had gained it:

Where now by Faith all arms are of a length;
One size doth all conditions fit.

A peasant may beleeve as much
As a great Clerk, and reach the highest stature.
Thus dost thou make proud knowledge bend & crouch,
While grace fills up uneven nature.

When creatures had no reall light
Inherent in them, thou didst make the sunne
Impute a lustre, and allow them bright;
And in this shew, what Christ hath done.

That which before was darkned clean
With bushie groves, pricking the lookers eie,
Vanisht away, when Faith did change the scene:
And then appear'd a glorious skie.

What though my bodie runne to dust?
Faith cleaves unto it, counting evr'y grain
With an exact and most particular trust,
Reserving all for flesh again.

Prayer [1]

Prayer the Churches banquet, Angels age,
Gods breath in man returning to his birth,
The soul in paraphrase, heart in pilgrimage,
The Christian plummet sounding heav'n and earth;
Engine against th' Almightie, sinners towre,
Reversed thunder, Christ-side-piercing spear,
The six-daies world transposing in an houre,
A kinde of tune, which all things heare and fear;

Softnesse, and peace, and joy, and love, and blisse,
    Exalted Manna, gladnesse of the best,
    Heaven in ordinarie, man well drest,
The milkie way, the bird of Paradise,
    Church-bels beyond the starres heard, the souls bloud,
    The land of spices; something understood.

The H. Communion

Not in rich furniture, or fine aray,
        Nor in a wedge of gold,
        Thou, who for me wast sold,
      To me dost now thy self convey;
For so thou should'st without me still have been,
        Leaving within me sinne:

But by the way of nourishment and strength
        Thou creep'st into my breast;
        Making thy way my rest,
      And thy small quantities my length;
Which spread their forces into every part,
        Meeting sinnes force and art.

Yet can these not get over to my soul,
          Leaping the wall that parts
          Our souls and fleshy hearts;
        But as th' outworks, they may controll
My rebel-flesh, and carrying thy name,
          Affright both sinne and shame.

Onely thy grace, which with these elements comes,
          Knoweth the ready way,
          And hath the privie key,

Op'ning the souls most subtile rooms;
While those to spirits refin'd, at doore attend
Dispatches from their friend.

Give me my captive soul, or take
My bodie also thither.
Another lift like this will make
Them both to be together.

Before that sinne turn'd flesh to stone,
And all our lump to leaven;
A fervent sigh might well have blown
Our innocent earth to heaven.

For sure when Adam did not know
To sinne, or sinne to smother;
He might to heav'n from Paradise go
As from one room t'another.

Thou hast restor'd us to this ease
By this thy heav'nly bloud;
Which I can go to, when I please,
And leave th' earth to their food.

The Temper [1]

How should I praise thee, Lord! how should my rymes
Gladly engrave thy love in steel,
If what my soul doth feel sometimes,
My soul might ever feel!

Although there were some fourtie heav'ns, or more,

Sometimes I peere above them all;
Sometimes I hardly reach a score,
Sometimes to hell I fall.

O rack me not to such a vast extent;
Those distances belong to thee:
The world's too little for thy tent,
A grave too big for me.

Wilt thou meet arms with man, that thou dost stretch
A crumme of dust from heav'n to hell?
Will great God measure with a wretch?
Shall he thy stature spell?

O let me, when thy roof my soul hath hid,
O let me roost and nestle there:
Then of a sinner thou art rid,
And I of hope and fear.

Yet take thy way; for sure thy way is best:
Stretch or contract me, thy poore debter:
This is but tuning of my breast,
To make the musick better.

Whether I flie with angels, fall with dust,
Thy hands made both, and I am there:
Thy power and love, my love and trust
Make one place ev'ry where.

Jordan [I]

Who sayes that fictions onely and false hair
Become a verse? Is there in truth no beautie?

Is all good structure in a winding stair?
May no lines passe, except they do their dutie
Not to a true, but painted chair?

Is it no verse, except enchanted groves
And sudden arbours shadow course-spunne lines?
Must purling streams refresh a lovers loves?
Must all be vail'd, while he that reades, divines,
Catching the sense at two removes?

Shepherds are honest people; let them sing:
Riddle who list, for me, and pull for Prime:
I envie no mans nightingale or spring;
Nor let them punish me with losse of rime,
Who plainly say, *My God, My King.*

Employment [I]

If as a flowre doth spread and die,
Thou wouldst extend me to some good,
Before I were by frosts extremitie
Nipt in the bud;

The sweetnesse and the praise were thine;
But the extension and the room,
Which in thy garland I should fill, were mine
At thy great doom.

For as thou dost impart thy grace,
The greater shall our glorie be.
The measure of our joyes is in this place,
The stuffe with thee.

Let me not languish then, and spend
A life as barren to thy praise,
As is the dust, to which that life doth tend,
But with delaies.

All things are busie; onely I
Neither bring hony with the bees,
Nor flowres to make that, nor the husbandrie
To water these.

I am no link of thy great chain,
But all my companie is a weed.
Lord place me in thy consort; give one strain
To my poore reed.

The H. Scriptures

I

Oh Book! infinite sweetnesse! let my heart
Suck ev'ry letter, and a hony gain,
Precious for any grief in any part;
To cleare the breast, to mollifie all pain.
Thou art all health, health thriving till it make
A full eternitie; thou art a masse
Of strange delights, where we may wish & take.
Ladies, look here; this is the thankfull glasse,
That mends the lookers eyes: this is the well
That washes what it shows. Who can indeare
Thy praise too much? thou art heav'ns Lidger here,
Working against the states of death and hell.
Thou art joyes handsell: heav'n lies flat in thee,
Subject to ev'ry mounters bended knee.

II

Oh that I knew how all thy lights combine,
    And the configurations of their glorie!
    Seeing not onely how each verse doth shine,
But all the constellations of the storie.
This verse marks that, and both do make a motion
    Unto a third, that ten leaves off doth lie:
    Then as dispersed herbs do watch a potion,
These three make up some Christians destinie:
Such are thy secrets, which my life makes good,
    And comments on thee: for in ev'ry thing
    Thy words do finde me out, & parallels bring,
And in another make me understood.
    Starres are poore books, & oftentimes do misse:
    This book of starres lights to eternall blisse.

Whitsunday

  Listen sweet Dove unto my song,
  And spread thy golden wings in me;
  Hatching my tender heart so long,
Till it get wing, and flie away with thee.

  Where is that fire which once descended
  On thy Apostles? thou didst then
  Keep open house, richly attended,
Feasting all comers by twelve chosen men.

  Such glorious gifts thou didst bestow,
  That th' earth did like a heav'n appeare;
  The starres were coming down to know
If they might mend their wages, and serve here.

The sunne, which once did shine alone,
Hung down his head, and wisht for night,
When he beheld twelve sunnes for one
Going about the world, and giving light.

But since those pipes of gold, which brought
That cordiall water to our ground,
Were cut and martyr'd by the fault
Of those, who did themselves through their side wound,

Thou shutt'st the doore, and keep'st within;
Scarce a good joy creeps through the chink:
And if the braves of conqu'ring sinne
Did not excite thee, we should wholly sink.

Lord, though we change, thou art the same;
The same sweet God of love and light:
Restore this day, for thy great name,
Unto his ancient and miraculous right.

Grace

My stock lies dead, and no increase
Doth my dull husbandrie improve:
O let thy graces without cease
Drop from above!

If still the sunne should hide his face,
Thy house would but a dungeon prove,
Thy works nights captives: O let grace
Drop from above!

The dew doth ev'ry morning fall;
And shall the dew out-strip thy Dove?
The dew, for which grasse cannot call,
Drop from above.

Death is still working like a mole,
And digs my grave at each remove:
Let grace work too, and on my soul
Drop from above.

Sinne is still hammering my heart
Unto a hardnesse, void of love:
Let suppling grace, to crosse his art,
Drop from above.

O come! for thou dost know the way:
Or if to me thou wilt not move,
Remove me, where I need not say,
Drop from above.

Praise [1]

To write a verse or two is all the praise,
That I can raise:
Mend my estate in any wayes,
Thou shalt have more.

I go to Church; help me to wings, and I
Will thither flie;
Or, if I mount unto the skie,
I will do more.

Man is all weaknesse; there is no such thing
As Prince or King:
His arm is short; yet with a sling
He may do more.

An herb destill'd, and drunk, may dwell next doore,
On the same floore,
To a brave soul: exalt the poore,
They can do more.

O raise me then! Poore bees, that work all day,
Sting my delay,
Who have a work, as well as they,
And much, much more.

Affliction [II]

Kill me not ev'ry day,
Thou Lord of life; since thy one death for me
Is more then all my deaths can be,
Though I in broken pay
Die over each houre of Methusalems stay.

If all mens tears were let
Into one common sewer, sea, and brine;
What were they all, compar'd to thine?
Wherein if they were set,
They would discolour thy most bloudy sweat.

Thou art my grief alone,
Thou Lord conceal it not: and as thou art
All my delight, so all my smart:
Thy crosse took up in one,
By way of imprest, all my future mone.

Mattens

I cannot ope mine eyes,
But thou art ready there to catch
My morning-soul and sacrifice:
Then we must needs for that day make a match.

My God, what is a heart?
Silver, or gold, or precious stone,
Or starre, or rainbow, or a part
Of all these things, or all of them in one?

My God, what is a heart,
That thou shouldst it so eye, and wooe,
Powring upon it all thy art,
As if that thou hadst nothing els to do?

Indeed mans whole estate
Amounts (and richly) to serve thee:
He did not heav'n and earth create,
Yet studies them, not him by whom they be.

Teach me thy love to know;
That this new light, which now I see,
May both the work and workman show:
Then by a sunne-beam I will climbe to thee.

Sinne [II]

O that I could a sinne once see!
We paint the devil foul, yet he
Hath some good in him, all agree.
Sinne is flat opposite to th' Almighty, seeing
It wants the good of *vertue,* and of *being.*

But God more care of us hath had:
If apparitions make us sad,
By sight of sinne we should grow mad.
Yet as in sleep we see foul death, and live:
So devils are our sinnes in perspective.

Even-song

Blest be the God of love,
Who gave me eyes, and light, and power this day,
Both to be busie, and to play.
But much more blest be God above,
Who gave me sight alone,
Which to himself he did denie:
For when he sees my waies, I dy:
But I have got his sonne, and he hath none.

What have I brought thee home
For this thy love? have I discharg'd the debt,
Which this dayes favour did beget?
I ranne; but all I brought, was fome.
Thy diet, care, and cost
Do end in bubbles, balls of winde;
Of winde to thee whom I have crost,
But balls of wilde-fire to my troubled minde.

Yet still thou goest on,
And now with darknesse closest wearie eyes,
Saying to man, *It doth suffice:*
Henceforth repose; your work is done.
Thus in thy ebony box
Thou dost inclose us, till the day
Put our amendment in our way,
And give new wheels to our disorder'd clocks.

I muse, which shows more love,
The day or night: that is the gale, this th' harbour;
That is the walk, and this the arbour;
Or that the garden, this the grove.
My God, thou art all love.
Not one poore minute scapes thy breast,
But brings a favour from above;
And in this love, more then in bed, I rest.

Church-monuments

While that my soul repairs to her devotion,
Here I intombe my flesh, that it betimes
May take acquaintance of this heap of dust;
To which the blast of deaths incessant motion,
Fed with the exhalation of our crimes,
Drives all at last. Therefore I gladly trust

My bodie to this school, that it may learn
To spell his elements, and finde his birth
Written in dustie heraldrie and lines;
Which dissolution sure doth best discern,
Comparing dust with dust, and earth with earth.
These laugh at Jeat and Marble put for signes,

To sever the good fellowship of dust,
And spoil the meeting. What shall point out them,
When they shall bow, and kneel, and fall down flat
To kisse those heaps, which now they have in trust?
Deare flesh, while I do pray, learn here thy stemme
And true descent; that when thou shalt grow fat,

And wanton in thy cravings, thou mayst know,
That flesh is but the glasse, which holds the dust

That measures all our time; which also shall
Be crumbled into dust. Mark here below
How tame these ashes are, how free from lust,
That thou mayst fit thy self against thy fall.

Church-musick

Sweetest of sweets, I thank you: when displeasure
Did through my bodie wound my minde,
You took me thence, and in your house of pleasure
A daintie lodging me assign'd.

Now I in you without a bodie move,
Rising and falling with your wings:
We both together sweetly live and love,
Yet say sometimes, *God help poore Kings.*

Comfort, I'le die; for if you poste from me,
Sure I shall do so, and much more:
But if I travell in your companie,
You know the way to heavens doore.

Church-lock and key

I Know it is my sinne, which locks thine eares,
And bindes thy hands,
Out-crying my requests, drowning my tears;
Or else the chilnesse of my faint demands.

But as cold hands are angrie with the fire,
And mend it still;
So I do lay the want of my desire,
Not on my sinnes, or coldnesse, but thy will.

Yet heare, O God, onely for his blouds sake
Which pleads for me:
For though sinnes plead too, yet like stones they make
His blouds sweet current much more loud to be.

The Church-floore

Mark you the floore? that square & speckled stone,
Which looks so firm and strong,
Is *Patience:*

And th' other black and grave, wherewith each one
Is checker'd all along,
Humilitie:

The gentle rising, which on either hand
Leads to the Quire above,
Is *Confidence:*

But the sweet cement, which in one sure band
Ties the whole frame, is *Love*
And *Charitie.*

Hither sometimes Sinne steals, and stains
The marbles neat and curious veins:
But all is cleansed when the marble weeps.
Sometimes Death, puffing at the doore,
Blows all the dust about the floore:
But while he thinks to spoil the room, he sweeps.
Blest be the *Architect,* whose art
Could build so strong in a weak heart.

The Windows

Lord, how can man preach thy eternall word?
He is a brittle crazie glasse:
Yet in thy temple thou dost him afford
This glorious and transcendent place,
To be a window, through thy grace.

But when thou dost anneal in glasse thy storie,
Making thy life to shine within
The holy Preachers; then the light and glorie
More rev'rend grows, & more doth win:
Which else shows watrish, bleak, & thin.

Doctrine and life, colours and light, in one
When they combine and mingle, bring
A strong regard and aw: but speech alone
Doth vanish like a flaring thing,
And in the eare, not conscience ring.

Trinitie Sunday

Lord, who hast form'd me out of mud,
And hast redeem'd me through thy bloud,
And sanctifi'd me to do good;

Purge all my sinnes done heretofore:
For I confesse my heavie score,
And I will strive to sinne no more.

Enrich my heart, mouth, hands in me,
With faith, with hope, with charitie;
That I may runne, rise, rest with thee.

Content

Peace mutt'ring thoughts, and do not grudge to keep
Within the walls of your own breast:
Who cannot on his own bed sweetly sleep,
Can on anothers hardly rest.

Gad not abroad at ev'ry quest and call
Of an untrained hope or passion.
To court each place or fortune that doth fall,
Is wantonnesse in contemplation.

Mark how the fire in flints doth quiet lie,
Content and warm t' it self alone:
But when it would appeare to others eye,
Without a knock it never shone.

Give me the pliant minde, whose gentle measure
Complies and suits with all estates;
Which can let loose to a crown, and yet with pleasure
Take up within a cloisters gates.

This soul doth span the world, and hang content
From either pole unto the centre:
Where in each room of the well-furnisht tent
He lies warm, and without adventure.

The brags of life are but a nine dayes wonder;
And after death the fumes that spring
From private bodies make as big a thunder,
As those which rise from a huge King.

Onely thy Chronicle is lost; and yet
Better by worms be all once spent,

Then to have hellish moths still gnaw and fret
Thy name in books, which may not rent:

When all thy deeds, whose brunt thou feel'st alone,
Are chaw'd by others pens and tongue;
And as their wit is, their digestion,
Thy nourisht fame is weak or strong.

Then cease discoursing soul, till thine own ground,
Do not thy self or friends importune.
He that by seeking hath himself once found,
Hath ever found a happie fortune.

The Quidditie

My God, a verse is not a crown,
No point of honour, or gay suit,
No hawk, or banquet, or renown,
Nor a good sword, nor yet a lute:

It cannot vault, or dance, or play;
It never was in *France* or *Spain;*
Nor can it entertain the day
With my great stable or demain:

It is no office, art, or news,
Nor the Exchange, or busie Hall;
But it is that which while I use
I am with thee, and *most take all.*

Humilitie

I saw the Vertues sitting hand in hand
In sev'rall ranks upon an azure throne,
Where all the beasts and fowl by their command
Presented tokens of submission.
Humilitie, who sat the lowest there
                    To execute their call,
When by the beasts the presents tendred were
                    Gave them about to all.

The angrie Lion did present his paw,
Which by consent was giv'n to Mansuetude.
The fearfull Hare her eares, which by their law
Humilitie did reach to Fortitude.
The jealous Turkie brought his corall-chain;
                    That went to Temperance.
On Justice was bestow'd the Foxes brain,
                    Kill'd in the way by chance.

At length the Crow bringing the Peacocks plume,
(For he would not) as they beheld the grace
Of that brave gift, each one began to fume,
And challenge it, as proper to his place,
Till they fell out: which when the beasts espied,
                    They leapt upon the throne;
And if the Fox had liv'd to rule their side,
                    They had depos'd each one.

Humilitie, who held the plume, at this
Did weep so fast, that the tears trickling down
Spoil'd all the train: then saying, *Here it is*
For which ye wrangle, made them turn their frown

Against the beasts: so joyntly bandying,
They drive them soon away;
And then amerc'd them, double gifts to bring
At the next Session-day.

Frailtie

Lord, in my silence how do I despise
What upon trust
Is styled *honour, riches,* or *fair eyes;*
But is *fair dust!*
I surname them *guilded clay,*
Deare earth, fine grasse or *hay;*
In all, I think my foot doth ever tread
Upon their head.

But when I view abroad both Regiments;
The worlds, and thine:
Thine clad with simplenesse, and sad events;
The other fine,
Full of glorie and gay weeds,
Brave language, braver deeds:
That which was dust before, doth quickly rise,
And prick mine eyes.

O brook not this, lest if what even now
My foot did tread,
Affront those joyes, wherewith thou didst endow
And long since wed
My poore soul, ev'n sick of love:
It may a Babel prove
Commodious to conquer heav'n and thee
Planted in me.

Affliction [III]

My heart did heave, and there came forth, *O God!*
By that I knew that thou wast in the grief,
To guide and govern it to my relief,
Making a scepter of the rod:
Hadst thou not had thy part,
Sure the unruly sigh had broke my heart.

But since thy breath gave me both life and shape,
Thou knowst my tallies; and when there's assign'd
So much breath to a sigh, what's then behinde?
Or if some yeares with it escape,
The sigh then onely is
A gale to bring me sooner to my blisse.

Thy life on earth was grief, and thou art still
Constant unto it, making it to be
A point of honour, now to grieve in me,
And in thy members suffer ill.
They who lament one crosse,
Thou dying dayly, praise thee to thy losse.

The Starre

Bright spark, shot from a brighter place,
Where beams surround my Saviours face,
Canst thou be any where
So well as there?

Yet, if thou wilt from thence depart,
Take a bad lodging in my heart;
For thou canst make a debter,
And make it better.

First with thy fire-work burn to dust
Folly, and worse then folly, lust:
Then with thy light refine,
And make it shine:

So disengag'd from sinne and sicknesse,
Touch it with thy celestiall quicknesse,
That it may hang and move
After thy love.

Then with our trinitie of light,
Motion, and heat, let's take our flight
Unto the place where thou
Before didst bow.

Get me a standing there, and place
Among the beams, which crown the face
Of him, who dy'd to part
Sinne and my heart:

That so among the rest I may
Glitter, and curle, and winde as they:
That winding is their fashion
Of adoration.

Sure thou wilt joy, by gaining me
To flie home like a laden bee
Unto that hive of beams
And garland-streams.

Sunday

O day most calm, most bright,
The fruit of this, the next worlds bud,

Th' indorsement of supreme delight,
Writ by a friend, and with his bloud;
The couch of time; cares balm and bay:
The week were dark, but for thy light:
        Thy torch doth show the way.

        The other dayes and thou
Make up one man; whose face thou art,
Knocking at heaven with thy brow:
The worky-daies are the back-part;
The burden of the week lies there,
Making the whole to stoup and bow,
        Till thy release appeare.

        Man had straight forward gone
To endlesse death: but thou dost pull
And turn us round to look on one,
Whom, if we were not very dull,
We could not choose but look on still;
Since there is no place so alone,
        The which he doth not fill.

        Sundaies the pillars are,
On which heav'ns palace arched lies:
The other dayes fill up the spare
And hollow room with vanities.
They are the fruitfull beds and borders
In Gods rich garden: that is bare,
        Which parts their ranks and orders.

        The Sundaies of mans life,
Thredded together on times string,
Make bracelets to adorn the wife
Of the eternall glorious King.
On Sunday heavens gate stands ope;

Blessings are plentifull and rife,
More plentifull then hope.

This day my Saviour rose,
And did inclose this light for his:
That, as each beast his manger knows,
Man might not of his fodder misse.
Christ hath took in this piece of ground,
And made a garden there for those
Who want herbs for their wound.

The rest of our Creation
Our great Redeemer did remove
With the same shake, which at his passion
Did th' earth and all things with it move.
As Sampson bore the doores away,
Christs hands, though nail'd, wrought our salvation,
And did unhinge that day.

The brightnesse of that day
We sullied by our foul offence:
Wherefore that robe we cast away,
Having a new at his expence,
Whose drops of bloud paid the full price,
That was requir'd to make us gay,
And fit for Paradise.

Thou art a day of mirth:
And where the week-dayes trail on ground,
Thy flight is higher, as thy birth.
O let me take thee at the bound,
Leaping with thee from sev'n to sev'n,
Till that we both, being toss'd from earth,
Flie hand in hand to heav'n!

Avarice

Money, thou bane of blisse, & sourse of wo,
  Whence com'st thou, that thou art so fresh and fine?
  I know thy parentage is base and low:
Man found thee poore and dirtie in a mine.
Surely thou didst so little contribute
  To this great kingdome, which thou now hast got,
  That he was fain, when thou wert destitute,
To digge thee out of thy dark cave and grot:
Then forcing thee by fire he made thee bright:
  Nay, thou hast got the face of man; for we
  Have with our stamp and seal transferr'd our right:
Thou art the man, and man but drosse to thee.
  Man calleth thee his wealth, who made thee rich;
  And while he digs out thee, falls in the ditch.

Ana- { MARY / ARMY } *gram*

How well her name an *Army* doth present,
In whom the *Lord of Hosts* did pitch his tent!

To all Angels and Saints

Oh glorious spirits, who after all your bands
See the smooth face of God without a frown
                    Or strict commands;
Where ev'ry one is king, and hath his crown,
If not upon his head, yet in his hands:

Not out of envie or maliciousnesse
Do I forbear to crave your speciall aid:
I would addresse
My vows to thee most gladly, Blessed Maid,
And Mother of my God, in my distresse.

Thou art the holy mine, whence came the gold,
The great restorative for all decay
In young and old;
Thou art the cabinet where the jewell lay:
Chiefly to thee would I my soul unfold:

But now, alas, I dare not; for our King,
Whom we do all joyntly adore and praise,
Bids no such thing:
And where his pleasure no injunction layes,
('Tis your own case) ye never move a wing.

All worship is prerogative, and a flower
Of his rich crown, from whom lyes no appeal
At the last houre:
Therefore we dare not from his garland steal,
To make a posie for inferiour power.

Although then others court you, if ye know
What's done on earth, we shall not fare the worse,
Who do not so;
Since we are ever ready to disburse,
If any one our Masters hand can show.

Employment [II]

He that is weary, let him sit.
My soul would stirre

And trade in courtesies and wit,
        Quitting the furre
To cold complexions needing it.

Man is no starre, but a quick coal
        Of mortall fire:
Who blows it not, nor doth controll
        A faint desire,
Lets his own ashes choke his soul.

When th' elements did for place contest
        With him, whose will
Ordain'd the highest to be best;
        The earth sat still,
And by the others is opprest.

Life is a businesse, not good cheer;
        Ever in warres.
The sunne still shineth there or here,
        Whereas the starres
Watch an advantage to appeare.

Oh that I were an Orenge-tree,
        That busie plant!
Then should I ever laden be,
        And never want
Some fruit for him that dressed me.

But we are still too young or old;
        The Man is gone,
Before we do our wares unfold:
        So we freeze on,
Until the grave increase our cold.

Deniall

When my devotions could not pierce
Thy silent eares;
Then was my heart broken, as was my verse:
My breast was full of fears
And disorder:

My bent thoughts, like a brittle bow,
Did flie asunder:
Each took his way; some would to pleasures go,
Some to the warres and thunder
Of alarms.

As good go any where, they say,
As to benumme
Both knees and heart, in crying night and day,
Come, come, my God, O come,
But no hearing.

O that thou shouldst give dust a tongue
To crie to thee,
And then not heare it crying! all day long
My heart was in my knee,
But no hearing.

Therefore my soul lay out of sight,
Untun'd, unstrung:
My feeble spirit, unable to look right,
Like a nipt blossome, hung
Discontented.

O cheer and tune my heartlesse breast,
Deferre no time;

That so thy favours granting my request,
They and my minde may chime,
And mend my ryme.

Christmas

All after pleasures as I rid one day,
My horse and I, both tir'd, bodie and minde,
With full crie of affections, quite astray,
I took up in the next inne I could finde.
There when I came, whom found I but my deare,
My dearest Lord, expecting till the grief
Of pleasures brought me to him, readie there
To be all passengers most sweet relief?
O Thou, whose glorious, yet contracted light,
Wrapt in nights mantle, stole into a manger;
Since my dark soul and brutish is thy right,
To Man of all beasts be not thou a stranger:
Furnish & deck my soul, that thou mayst have
A better lodging then a rack or grave.

The shepherds sing; and shall I silent be?
My God, no hymne for thee?
My soul's a shepherd too; a flock it feeds
Of thoughts, and words, and deeds.
The pasture is thy word: the streams, thy grace
Enriching all the place.
Shepherd and flock shall sing, and all my powers
Out-sing the day-light houres.
Then we will chide the sunne for letting night
Take up his place and right:
We sing one common Lord; wherefore he should

Himself the candle hold.
I will go searching, till I finde a sunne
Shall stay, till we have done;
A willing shiner, that shall shine as gladly,
As frost-nipt sunnes look sadly.
Then we will sing, and shine all our own day,
And one another pay:
His beams shall cheer my breast, and both so twine,
Till ev'n his beams sing, and my musick shine.

Ungratefulnesse

Lord, with what bountie and rare clemencie
Hast thou redeem'd us from the grave!
If thou hadst let us runne,
Gladly had man ador'd the sunne,
And thought his god most brave;
Where now we shall be better gods then he.

Thou hast but two rare cabinets full of treasure,
The *Trinitie,* and *Incarnation:*
Thou hast unlockt them both,
And made them jewels to betroth
The work of thy creation
Unto thy self in everlasting pleasure.

The statelier cabinet is the *Trinitie,*
Whose sparkling light accesse denies:
Therefore thou dost not show
This fully to us, till death blow
The dust into our eyes:
For by that powder thou wilt make us see.

But all thy sweets are packt up in the other;
Thy mercies thither flock and flow:
That as the first affrights,
This may allure us with delights;
Because this box we know;
For we have all of us just such another.

But man is close, reserv'd, and dark to thee:
When thou demandest but a heart,
He cavils instantly.
In his poore cabinet of bone
Sinnes have their box apart,
Defrauding thee, who gavest two for one.

Sighs and Grones

O do not use me
After my sinnes! look not on my desert,
But on thy glorie! then thou wilt reform
And not refuse me: for thou onely art
The mightie God, but I a sillie worm;
O do not bruise me!

O do not urge me!
For what account can thy ill steward make?
I have abus'd thy stock, destroy'd thy woods,
Suckt all thy magazens: my head did ake,
Till it found out how to consume thy goods:
O do not scourge me!

O do not blinde me!
I have deserv'd that an Egyptian night
Should thicken all my powers; because my lust

Hath still sow'd fig-leaves to exclude thy light:
But I am frailtie, and already dust;
O do not grinde me!

O do not fill me
With the turn'd viall of thy bitter wrath!
For thou hast other vessels full of bloud,
A part whereof my Saviour empti'd hath,
Ev'n unto death: since he di'd for my good,
O do not kill me!

But O reprieve me!
For thou hast life and death at thy command;
Thou art both *Judge* and *Saviour, feast* and *rod,*
Cordiall and *Corrosive:* put not thy hand
Into the bitter box; but O my God,
My God, relieve me!

The World

Love built a stately house; where *Fortune* came,
And spinning phansies, she was heard to say,
That her fine cobwebs did support the frame,
Whereas they were supported by the same:
But *Wisdome* quickly swept them all away.

Then *Pleasure* came, who, liking not the fashion,
Began to make *Balcones, Terraces,*
Till she had weakened all by alteration:
But rev'rend *laws,* and many a *proclamation*
Reformed all at length with menaces.

The enter'd *Sinne,* and with that Sycomore,

Whose leaves first sheltered man from drought & dew,
Working and winding slily evermore,
The inward walls and sommers cleft and tore:
But *Grace* shor'd these, and cut that as it grew.

Then *Sinne* combin'd with *Death* in a firm band
To raze the building to the very floore:
Which they effected, none could them withstand.
But *Love* and *Grace* took *Glorie* by the hand,
And built a braver Palace then before.

Coloss. 3. 3

OUR LIFE IS HID WITH CHRIST IN GOD

My words & thoughts do both expresse this notion,
That *Life* hath with the sun a double motion.
The first *Is* straight, and our diurnall friend,
The other *Hid* and doth obliquely bend.
One life is wrapt *In* flesh, and tends to earth:
The other winds towards *Him,* whose happie birth
Taught me to live here so, *That* still one eye
Should aim and shoot at that which *Is* on high:
Quitting with daily labour all *My* pleasure,
To gain at harvest an eternall *Treasure.*

Vanitie [1]

The fleet Astronomer can bore,
And thred the spheres with his quick-piercing minde:
He views their stations, walks from doore to doore,
Surveys, as if he had design'd

To make a purchase there: he sees their dances,
And knoweth long before
Both their full-ey'd aspects, and secret glances.

The nimble Diver with his side
Cuts through the working waves, that he may fetch
His dearely-earned pearl, which God did hide
On purpose from the ventrous wretch;
That he might save his life, and also hers,
Who with excessive pride
Her own destruction and his danger wears.

The subtil Chymick can devest
And strip the creature naked, till he finde
The callow principles within their nest:
There he imparts to them his minde,
Admitted to their bed-chamber, before
They appeare trim and drest
To ordinarie suitours at the doore.

What hath not man sought out and found,
But his deare God? who yet his glorious law
Embosomes in us, mellowing the ground
With showres and frosts, with love & aw,
So that we need not say, Where's this command?
Poore man, thou searchest round
To finde out *death,* but missest *life* at hand.

Vertue

Sweet day, so cool, so calm, so bright,
The bridall of the earth and skie:
The dew shall weep thy fall to night;
For thou must die.

Sweet rose, whose hue angrie and brave
Bids the rash gazer wipe his eye:
Thy root is ever in its grave,
And thou must die.

Sweet spring, full of sweet dayes and roses,
A box where sweets compacted lie;
My musick shows ye have your closes,
And all must die.

Onely a sweet and vertuous soul,
Like season'd timber, never gives;
But though the whole world turn to coal,
Then chiefly lives.

The Pearl. Matt. 13. 45

I know the wayes of Learning; both the head
And pipes that feed the presse, and make it runne;
What reason hath from nature borrowed,
Or of it self, like a good huswife, spunne
In laws and policie; what the starres conspire,
What willing nature speaks, what forc'd by fire;
Both th' old discoveries, and the new-found seas,
The stock and surplus, cause and historie:
All these stand open, or I have the keyes:
Yet I love thee.

I know the wayes of Honour, what maintains
The quick returns of courtesie and wit:
In vies of favours whether partie gains,
When glorie swells the heart, and moldeth it
To all expressions both of hand and eye,
Which on the world a true-love-knot may tie,

And bear the bundle, wheresoe're it goes;
How many drammes of spirit there must be
To sell my life unto my friends or foes:
Yet I love thee.

I know the wayes of Pleasure, the sweet strains,
The lullings and the relishes of it;
The propositions of hot bloud and brains;
What mirth and musick mean; what love and wit
Have done these twentie hundred yeares, and more:
I know the projects of unbridled store:
My stuffe is flesh, not brasse; my senses live,
And grumble oft, that they have more in me
Then he that curbs them, being but one to five:
Yet I love thee.

I know all these, and have them in my hand:
Therefore not sealed, but with open eyes
I flie to thee, and fully understand
Both the main sale, and the commodities;
And at what rate and price I have thy love;
With all the circumstances that may move:
Yet through these labyrinths, not my groveling wit,
But thy silk twist let down from heav'n to me,
Did both conduct and teach me, how by it
To climbe to thee.

Affliction [IV]

Broken in pieces all asunder,
Lord, hunt me not,
A thing forgot,

Once a poore creature, now a wonder,
    A wonder tortur'd in the space
    Betwixt this world and that of grace.

My thoughts are all a case of knives,
        Wounding my heart
        With scatter'd smart,
As watring pots give flowers their lives.
    Nothing their furie can controll,
    While they do wound and pink my soul.

All my attendants are at strife,
        Quitting their place
        Unto my face:
Nothing performs the task of life:
    The elements are let loose to fight,
    And while I live, trie out their right.

Oh help, my God! let not their plot
        Kill them and me,
        And also thee,
Who art my life: dissolve the knot,
    As the sunne scatters by his light
    All the rebellions of the night.

Then shall those powers, which work for grief,
        Enter thy pay,
        And day by day
Labour thy praise, and my relief;
    With care and courage building me,
    Till I reach heav'n, and much more, thee.

Man

My God, I heard this day,
That none doth build a stately habitation,
But he that means to dwell therein.
What house more stately hath there been,
Or can be, then is Man? to whose creation
All things are in decay.

For Man is ev'ry thing,
And more: He is a tree, yet bears more fruit;
A beast, yet is, or should be more:
Reason and speech we onely bring.
Parrats may thank us, if they are not mute,
They go upon the score.

Man is all symmetrie,
Full of proportions, one limbe to another,
And all to all the world besides:
Each part may call the furthest, brother:
For head with foot hath private amitie,
And both with moons and tides.

Nothing hath got so farre,
But Man hath caught and kept it, as his prey.
His eyes dismount the highest starre:
He is in little all the sphere.
Herbs gladly cure our flesh; because that they
Finde their acquaintance there.

For us the windes do blow,
The earth doth rest, heav'n move, and fountains flow.
Nothing we see, but means our good,

As our delight, or as our treasure:
The whole is, either our cupboard of food,
Or cabinet of pleasure.

The starres have us to bed;
Night draws the curtain, which the sunne withdraws;
Musick and light attend our head.
All things unto our flesh are kinde
In their descent and being; to our minde
In their ascent and cause.

Each thing is full of dutie:
Waters united are our navigation;
Distinguished, our habitation;
Below, our drink; above, our meat;
Both are our cleanlinesse. Hath one such beautie?
Then how are all things neat?

More servants wait on Man,
Then he'l take notice of: in ev'ry path
He treads down that which doth befriend him,
When sicknesse makes him pale and wan.
Oh mightie love! Man is one world, and hath
Another to attend him.

Since then, my God, thou hast
So brave a Palace built; O dwell in it,
That it may dwell with thee at last!
Till then, afford us so much wit;
That, as the world serves us, we may serve thee,
And both thy servants be.

Antiphon [II]

Chor. Praised be the God of love,
Men. Here below,
Angels. And here above:
Cho. Who hath dealt his mercies so,
Ang. To his friend,
Men. And to his foe;

Cho. That both grace and glorie tend
Ang. Us of old,
Men. And us in th'end.
Cho. The great shepherd of the fold
Ang. Us did make,
Men. For us was sold.
Cho. He our foes in pieces brake;
Ang. Him we touch;
Men. And him we take.
Cho. Wherefore since that he is such,
Ang. We adore,
Men. And we do crouch.

Cho. Lord, thy praises should be more.
Men. We have none,
Ang. And we no store.
Cho. Praised be the God alone,
Who hath made of two folds one.

Unkindnesse

Lord, make me coy and tender to offend:
In friendship, first I think, if that agree,
Which I intend,

Unto my friends intent and end.
I would not use a friend, as I use Thee.

If any touch my friend, or his good name,
It is my honour and my love to free
His blasted fame
From the least spot or thought of blame.
I could not use a friend, as I use Thee.

My friend may spit upon my curious floore:
Would he have gold? I lend it instantly;
But let the poore,
And thou within them, starve at doore.
I cannot use a friend, as I use Thee.

When that my friend pretendeth to a place,
I quit my interest, and leave it free:
But when thy grace
Sues for my heart, I thee displace,
Nor would I use a friend, as I use Thee.

Yet can a friend what thou hast done fulfill?
O write in brasse, *My God upon a tree*
His bloud did spill
Onely to purchase my good-will.
Yet use I not my foes, as I use Thee.

Life

I made a posie, while the day ran by:
Here will I smell my remnant out, and tie
My life within this band.
But Time did becken to the flowers, and they

By noon most cunningly did steal away,
And wither'd in my hand.

My hand was next to them, and then my heart:
I took, without more thinking, in good part
Times gentle admonition:
Who did so sweetly deaths sad taste convey,
Making my minde to smell my fatall day;
Yet sugring the suspicion.

Farewell deare flowers, sweetly your time ye spent,
Fit, while ye liv'd, for smell or ornament,
And after death for cures.
I follow straight without complaints or grief,
Since if my sent be good, I care not if
It be as short as yours.

Justice [1]

I cannot skill of these thy wayes.
Lord, thou didst make me, yet thou woundest me;
Lord, thou dost wound me, yet thou dost relieve me:
Lord, thou relievest, yet I die by thee:
Lord, thou dost kill me, yet thou dost reprieve me.

But when I mark my life and praise,
Thy justice me most fitly payes:
For, *I do praise thee, yet I praise thee not:*
My prayers mean thee, yet my prayers stray:
I would do well, yet sinne the hand hath got:
My soul doth love thee, yet it loves delay.
I cannot skill of these my wayes.

Charms and Knots

Who reade a chapter when they rise,
Shall ne're be troubled with ill eyes.

A poore mans rod, when thou dost ride,
Is both a weapon and a guide.

Who shuts his hand, hath lost his gold:
Who opens it, hath it twice told.

Who goes to bed and does not pray,
Maketh two nights to ev'ry day.

Who by aspersions throw a stone
At th' head of others, hit their own.

Who looks on ground with humble eyes,
Findes himself there, and seeks to rise.

When th' hair is sweet through pride or lust,
The powder doth forget the dust.

Take one from ten, and what remains?
Ten still, if sermons go for gains.

In shallow waters heav'n doth show;
But who drinks on, to hell may go.

Affliction [v]

My God, I read this day,
That planted Paradise was not so firm,

As was and is thy floting Ark; whose stay
And anchor thou art onely, to confirm
And strengthen it in ev'ry age,
When waves do rise, and tempests rage.

At first we liv'd in pleasure;
Thine own delights thou didst to us impart:
When we grew wanton, thou didst use displeasure
To make us thine: yet that we might not part,
As we at first did board with thee,
Now thou wouldst taste our miserie.

There is but joy and grief;
If either will convert us, we are thine:
Some Angels us'd the first; if our relief
Take up the second, then thy double line
And sev'rall baits in either kinde
Furnish thy table to thy minde.

Affliction then is ours;
We are the trees, whom shaking fastens more,
While blustring windes destroy the wanton bowres,
And ruffle all their curious knots and store.
My God, so temper joy and wo,
That thy bright beams may tame thy bow.

Mortification

How soon doth man decay!
When clothes are taken from a chest of sweets
To swaddle infants, whose young breath
Scarce knows the way;
Those clouts are little winding sheets,
Which do consigne and send them unto death.

When boyes go first to bed,
They step into their voluntarie graves,
Sleep bindes them fast; onely their breath
Makes them not dead:
Successive nights, like rolling waves,
Convey them quickly, who are bound for death.

When youth is frank and free,
And calls for musick, while his veins do swell,
All day exchanging mirth and breath
In companie;
That musick summons to the knell,
Which shall befriend him at the houre of death.

When man grows staid and wise,
Getting a house and home, where he may move
Within the circle of his breath,
Schooling his eyes;
That dumbe inclosure maketh love
Unto the coffin, that attends his death.

When age grows low and weak,
Marking his grave, and thawing ev'ry yeare,
Till all do melt, and drown his breath
When he would speak;
A chair or litter shows the biere,
Which shall convey him to the house of death.

Man, ere he is aware,
Hath put together a solemnitie,
And drest his herse, while he has breath
As yet to spare:
Yet Lord, instruct us so to die,
That all these dyings may be life in death.

Decay

Sweet were the dayes, when thou didst lodge with Lot,
Struggle with Jacob, sit with Gideon,
Advise with Abraham, when thy power could not
Encounter Moses strong complaints and mone:
  Thy words were then, *Let me alone.*

One might have sought and found thee presently
At some fair oak, or bush, or cave, or well:
Is my God this way? No, they would reply:
He is to Sinai gone, as we heard tell:
  List, ye may heare great Aarons bell.

But now thou dost thy self immure and close
In some one corner of a feeble heart:
Where yet both Sinne and Satan, thy old foes,
Do pinch and straiten thee, and use much art
  To gain thy thirds and little part.

I see the world grows old, when as the heat
Of thy great love, once spread, as in an urn
Doth closet up it self, and still retreat,
Cold Sinne still forcing it, till it return,
  And calling *Justice,* all things burn.

Miserie

Lord, let the Angels praise thy name.
Man is a foolish thing, a foolish thing,
Folly and Sinne play all his game.
His house still burns, and yet he still doth sing,
Man is but grasse,
He knows it, fill the glasse.

How canst thou brook his foolishnesse?
Why, he'l not lose a cup of drink for thee:
Bid him but temper his excesse;
Not he: he knows where he can better be,
As he will swear,
Then to serve thee in fear.

What strange pollutions doth he wed,
And make his own? as if none knew but he.
No man shall beat into his head,
That thou within his curtains drawn canst see:
They are of cloth,
Where never yet came moth.

The best of men, turn but thy hand
For one poore minute, stumble at a pinne:
They would not have their actions scann'd,
Nor any sorrow tell them that they sinne,
Though it be small,
And measure not their fall.

They quarrell thee, and would give over
The bargain made to serve thee: but thy love
Holds them unto it, and doth cover
Their follies with the wing of thy milde Dove,
Not suff'ring those
Who would, to be thy foes.

My God, Man cannot praise thy name:
Thou art all brightnesse, perfect puritie;
The sunne holds down his head for shame,
Dead with eclipses, when we speak of thee:
How shall infection
Presume on thy perfection?

As dirtie hands foul all they touch,
And those things most, which are most pure and fine:
So our clay hearts, ev'n when we crouch
To sing thy praises, make them lesse divine.
Yet either this,
Or none, thy portion is.

Man cannot serve thee; let him go,
And serve the swine: there, there is his delight:
He does not like this vertue, no;
Give him his dirt to wallow in all night:
These Preachers make
His head to shoot and ake.

Oh foolish man! where are thine eyes?
How hast thou lost them in a croud of cares?
Thou pull'st the rug, and wilt not rise,
No, not to purchase the whole pack of starres:
There let them shine,
Thou must go sleep, or dine.

The bird that sees a daintie bowre
Made in the tree, where she was wont to sit,
Wonders and sings, but not his power
Who made the arbour: this exceeds her wit.
But Man doth know
The spring, whence all things flow:

And yet, as though he knew it not,
His knowledge winks, and lets his humours reigne;
They make his life a constant blot,
And all the bloud of God to run in vain.
Ah wretch! what verse
Can thy strange wayes rehearse?

Indeed at first Man was a treasure,
A box of jewels, shop of rarities,
A ring, whose posie was, *My pleasure:*
He was a garden in a Paradise:
Glorie and grace
Did crown his heart and face.

But sinne hath fool'd him. Now he is
A lump of flesh, without a foot or wing
To raise him to a glimpse of blisse:
A sick toss'd vessel, dashing on each thing;
Nay, his own shelf:
My God, I mean my self.

Jordan [II]

When first my lines of heav'nly joyes made mention,
Such was their lustre, they did so excell,
That I sought out quaint words, and trim invention;
My thoughts began to burnish, sprout, and swell,
Curling with metaphors a plain intention,
Decking the sense, as if it were to sell.

Thousands of notions in my brain did runne,
Off'ring their service, if I were not sped:
I often blotted what I had begunne;
This was not quick enough, and that was dead.
Nothing could seem too rich to clothe the sunne,
Much lesse those joyes which trample on his head.

As flames do work and winde, when they ascend,
So did I weave my self into the sense.
But while I bustled, I might heare a friend

Whisper, *How wide is all this long pretence!*
There is in love a sweetnesse readie penn'd:
Copie out onely that, and save expense.

Obedience

My God, if writings may
Convey a Lordship any way
Whither the buyer and the seller please;
Let it not thee displease,
If this poore paper do as much as they.

On it my heart doth bleed
As many lines, as there doth need
To passe it self and all it hath to thee.
To which I do agree,
And here present it as my speciall Deed.

If that hereafter Pleasure
Cavill, and claim her part and measure,
As if this passed with a reservation,
Or some such words in fashion;
I here exclude the wrangler from thy treasure.

O let thy sacred will
All thy delight in me fulfill!
Let me not think an action mine own way,
But as thy love shall sway,
Resigning up the rudder to thy skill.

Lord, what is man to thee,
That thou shouldst minde a rotten tree?
Yet since thou canst not choose but see my actions;

So great are thy perfections,
Thou mayst as well my actions guide, as see.

Besides, thy death and bloud
Show'd a strange love to all our good:
Thy sorrows were in earnest; no faint proffer,
Or superficiall offer
Of what we might not take, or be withstood.

Wherefore I all forgo:
To one word onely I say, No:
Where in the Deed there was an intimation
Of a gift or donation,
Lord, let it now by way of purchase go.

He that will passe his land,
As I have mine, may set his hand
And heart unto this Deed, when he hath read;
And make the purchase spread
To both our goods, if he to it will stand.

How happie were my part,
If some kinde man would thrust his heart
Into these lines; till in heav'ns Court of Rolls
They were by winged souls
Entred for both, farre above their desert!

Sion

Lord, with what glorie wast thou serv'd of old,
When Solomons temple stood and flourished!
Where most things were of purest gold;
The wood was all embellished

With flowers and carvings, mysticall and rare:
All show'd the builders, crav'd the seeers care.

Yet all this glorie, all this pomp and state
Did not affect thee much, was not thy aim;
    Something there was, that sow'd debate:
    Wherefore thou quitt'st thy ancient claim:
And now thy Architecture meets with sinne;
For all thy frame and fabrick is within.

There thou art struggling with a peevish heart,
Which sometimes crosseth thee, thou sometimes it:
    The fight is hard on either part.
    Great God doth fight, he doth submit.
All Solomons sea of brasse and world of stone
Is not so deare to thee as one good grone.

And truly brasse and stones are heavie things,
Tombes for the dead, not temples fit for thee:
    But grones are quick, and full of wings,
    And all their motions upward be;
And ever as they mount, like larks they sing;
The note is sad, yet musick for a King.

The British Church

I joy, deare Mother, when I view
Thy perfect lineaments and hue
                    Both sweet and bright.
Beautie in thee takes up her place,
And dates her letters from thy face,
                    When she doth write.

A fine aspect in fit aray,
Neither too mean, nor yet too gay,
Shows who is best.
Outlandish looks may not compare:
For all they either painted are,
Or else undrest.

She on the hills, which wantonly
Allureth all in hope to be
By her preferr'd,
Hath kiss'd so long her painted shrines,
That ev'n her face by kissing shines,
For her reward.

She in the valley is so shie
Of dressing, that her hair doth lie
About her eares:
While she avoids her neighbours pride,
She wholly goes on th' other side,
And nothing wears.

But dearest Mother, what those misse,
The mean, thy praise and glorie is,
And long may be.
Blessed be God, whose love it was
To double-moat thee with his grace,
And none but thee.

The Quip

The merrie world did on a day
With his train-bands and mates agree

To meet together, where I lay,
And all in sport to geere at me.

First, Beautie crept into a rose,
Which when I pluckt not, Sir, said she,
Tell me, I pray, Whose hands are those?
But thou shalt answer, Lord, for me.

Then Money came, and chinking still,
What tune is this, poore man? said he:
I heard in Musick you had skill.
But thou shalt answer, Lord, for me.

Then came brave Glorie puffing by
In silks that whistled, who but he?
He scarce allow'd me half an eie.
But thou shalt answer, Lord, for me.

Then came quick Wit and Conversation,
And he would needs a comfort be,
And, to be short, make an Oration.
But thou shalt answer, Lord, for me.

Yet when the houre of thy designe
To answer these fine things shall come;
Speak not at large; say, I am thine:
And then they have their answer home.

Vanitie [II]

Poore silly soul, whose hope and head lies low;
Whose flat delights on earth do creep and grow;
To whom the starres shine not so fair, as eyes;

Nor solid work, as false embroyderies;
Heark and beware, lest what you now do measure
And write for sweet, prove a most sowre displeasure.

O heare betimes, lest thy relenting
May come too late!
To purchase heaven for repenting
Is no hard rate.
If souls be made of earthly mold,
Let them love gold;
If born on high,
Let them unto their kindred flie:
For they can never be at rest,
Till they regain their ancient nest.
Then silly soul take heed; for earthly joy
Is but a bubble, and makes thee a boy.

The Dawning

Awake sad heart, whom sorrow ever drowns;
Take up thine eyes, which feed on earth;
Unfold thy forehead gather'd into frowns:
Thy Saviour comes, and with him mirth:
Awake, awake;
And with a thankfull heart his comforts take.
But thou dost still lament, and pine, and crie;
And feel his death, but not his victorie.

Arise sad heart; if thou doe not withstand,
Christs resurrection thine may be:
Do not by hanging down break from the hand,
Which as it riseth, raiseth thee:

Arise, arise;
And with his buriall-linen drie thine eyes:
Christ left his grave-clothes, that we might, when grief
Draws tears, or bloud, not want a handkerchief.

JESU

Jesu is in my heart, his sacred name
Is deeply carved there: but th' other week
A great affliction broke the little frame,
Ev'n all to pieces: which I went to seek:
And first I found the corner, where was *J*,
After, where *ES*, and next there *U* was graved.
When I had got these parcels, instantly
I sat me down to spell them, and perceived
That to my broken heart he was *I ease you*,
And to my whole is *JESU*.

Businesse

Canst be idle? canst thou play,
Foolish soul who sinn'd to day?

Rivers run, and springs each one
Know their home, and get them gone:
Hast thou tears, or hast thou none?

If, poore soul, thou hast no tears,
Would thou hadst no faults or fears!
Who hath these, those ill forbears.

Windes still work: it is their plot,
Be the season cold, or hot:
Hast thou sighs, or hast thou not?

If thou hast no sighs or grones,
Would thou hadst no flesh and bones!
Lesser pains scape greater ones.

But if yet thou idle be,
Foolish soul, Who di'd for thee?

Who did leave his Fathers throne,
To assume thy flesh and bone;
Had he life, or had he none?

If he had not liv'd for thee,
Thou hadst di'd most wretchedly;
And two deaths had been thy fee.

He so farre thy good did plot,
That his own self he forgot.
Did he die, or did he not?

If he had not di'd for thee,
Thou hadst liv'd in miserie.
Two lives worse then ten deaths be.

And hath any space of breath
'Twixt his sinnes and Saviours death?

He that loseth gold, though drosse,
Tells to all he meets, his crosse:
He that sinnes, hath he no losse?

He that findes a silver vein,
Thinks on it, and thinks again:
Brings thy Saviours death no gain?

        Who in heart not ever kneels,
        Neither sinne nor Saviour feels.

Dialogue

Sweetest Saviour, if my soul
    Were but worth the having,
Quickly should I then controll
    Any thought of waving.
But when all my care and pains
Cannot give the name of gains
To thy wretch so full of stains,
What delight or hope remains?

What, Child, is the ballance thine,
    Thine the poise and measure?
If I say, Thou shalt be mine;
    Finger not my treasure.
What the gains in having thee
Do amount to, onely he,
Who for man was sold, can see;
That transferr'd th' accounts to me.

But as I can see no merit,
    Leading to this favour:
So the way to fit me for it
    Is beyond my savour.
As the reason then is thine;
So the way is none of mine:

I disclaim the whole designe;
Sinne disclaims and I resigne.

That is all, if that I could
Get without repining;
And my clay, my creature, would
Follow my resigning:
That as I did freely part
With my glorie and desert,
Left all joyes to feel all smart——
Ah! no more: thou break'st my heart.

Dulnesse

Why do I languish thus, drooping and dull,
As if I were all earth?
O give me quicknesse, that I may with mirth
Praise thee brim-full!

The wanton lover in a curious strain
Can praise his fairest fair;
And with quaint metaphors her curled hair
Curl o're again.

Thou art my lovelinesse, my life, my light,
Beautie alone to me:
Thy bloudy death and undeserv'd, makes thee
Pure red and white.

When all perfections as but one appeare,
That those thy form doth show,
The very dust, where thou dost tread and go,
Makes beauties here.

Where are my lines then? my approaches? views?
Where are my window-songs?
Lovers are still pretending, & ev'n wrongs
Sharpen their Muse:

But I am lost in flesh, whose sugred lyes
Still mock me, and grow bold:
Sure thou didst put a minde there, if I could
Finde where it lies.

Lord, cleare thy gift, that with a constant wit
I may but look towards thee:
Look onely; for to *love* thee, who can be,
What angel fit?

Love-joy

As on a window late I cast mine eye,
I saw a vine drop grapes with *J* and *C*
Anneal'd on every bunch. One standing by
Ask'd what it meant. I, who am never loth
To spend my judgement, said, It seem'd to me
To be the bodie and the letters both
Of *Joy* and *Charitie.* Sir, you have not miss'd,
The man reply'd; It figures *JESUS CHRIST*.

Providence

O sacred Providence, who from end to end
Strongly and sweetly movest, shall I write,
And not of thee, through whom my fingers bend
To hold my quill? shall they not do thee right?

Of all the creatures both in sea and land
Onely to Man thou hast made known thy wayes.
And put the penne alone into his hand,
And made him Secretarie of thy praise.

Beasts fain would sing; birds dittie to their notes;
Trees would be tuning on their native lute
To thy renown: but all their hands and throats
Are brought to Man, while they are lame and mute.

Man is the worlds high Priest: he doth present
The sacrifice for all; while they below
Unto the service mutter an assent,
Such as springs use that fall, and windes that blow.

He that to praise and laud thee doth refrain,
Doth not refrain unto himself alone,
But robs a thousand who would praise thee fain,
And doth commit a world of sinne in one.

The beasts say, Eat me: but, if beasts must teach,
The tongue is yours to eat, but mine to praise.
The trees say, Pull me: but the hand you stretch,
Is mine to write, as it is yours to raise.

Wherefore, most sacred Spirit, I here present
For me and all my fellows praise to thee:
And just it is that I should pay the rent,
Because the benefit accrues to me.

We all acknowledge both thy power and love
To be exact, transcendent, and divine;
Who dost so strongly and so sweetly move,
While all things have their will, yet none but thine.

For either thy command or thy permission
Lay hands on all: they are thy right and left.
The first puts on with speed and expedition;
The other curbs sinnes stealing pace and theft.

Nothing escapes them both; all must appeare,
And be dispos'd, and dress'd, and tun'd by thee,
Who sweetly temper'st all. If we could heare
Thy skill and art, what musick would it be!

Thou art in small things great, not small in any:
Thy even praise can neither rise, nor fall.
Thou art in all things one, in each thing many:
For thou art infinite in one and all.

Tempests are calm to thee; they know thy hand,
And hold it fast, as children do their fathers,
Which crie and follow. Thou hast made poore sand
Check the proud sea, ev'n when it swells and gathers.

Thy cupboard serves the world: the meat is set,
Where all may reach: no beast but knows his feed.
Birds teach us hawking; fishes have their net:
The great prey on the lesse, they on some weed.

Nothing ingendred doth prevent his meat:
Flies have their table spread, ere they appeare.
Some creatures have in winter what to eat;
Others do sleep, and envie not their cheer.

How finely dost thou times and seasons spin,
And make a twist checker'd with night and day!
Which as it lengthens windes, and windes us in,
As bouls go on, but turning all the way.

Each creature hath a wisdome for his good.
The pigeons feed their tender off-spring, crying,
When they are callow; but withdraw their food
When they are fledge, that need may teach them flying.

Bees work for man; and yet they never bruise
Their masters flower, but leave it, having done,
As fair as ever, and as fit to use;
So both the flower doth stay, and hony run.

Sheep eat the grasse, and dung the ground for more:
Trees after bearing drop their leaves for soil:
Springs vent their streams, and by expense get store:
Clouds cool by heat, and baths by cooling boil.

Who hath the vertue to expresse the rare
And curious vertues both of herbs and stones?
Is there an herb for that? Or that thy care
Would show a root, that gives expressions!

And if an herb hath power, what have the starres?
A rose, besides his beautie, is a cure.
Doubtlesse our plagues and plentie, peace and warres
Are there much surer then our art is sure.

Thou hast hid metals: man may take them thence;
But at his perill: when he digs the place,
He makes a grave; as if the thing had sense,
And threatned man, that he should fill the space.

Ev'n poysons praise thee. Should a thing be lost?
Should creatures want for want of heed their due?
Since where are poysons, antidotes are most:
The help stands close, and keeps the fear in view.

The sea, which seems to stop the traveller,
Is by a ship the speedier passage made.
The windes, who think they rule the mariner,
Are rul'd by him, and taught to serve his trade.

And as thy house is full, so I adore
Thy curious art in marshalling thy goods.
The hills with health abound; the vales with store;
The South with marble; North with furres & woods.

Hard things are glorious; easie things good cheap.
The common all men have; that which is rare
Men therefore seek to have, and care to keep.
The healthy frosts with summer-fruits compare.

Light without winde is glasse: warm without weight
Is wooll and furre: cool without closenesse, shade:
Speed without pains, a horse: tall without height,
A servile hawk: low without losse, a spade.

All countreys have enough to serve their need:
If they seek fine things, thou dost make them run
For their offence; and then dost turn their speed
To be commerce and trade from sunne to sunne.

Nothing wears clothes, but Man; nothing doth need
But he to wear them. Nothing useth fire,
But Man alone, to show his heav'nly breed:
And onely he hath fuell in desire.

When th' earth was dry, thou mad'st a sea of wet:
When that lay gather'd, thou didst broach the mountains:
When yet some places could no moisture get,
The windes grew gard'ners, and the clouds good fountains.

Rain, do not hurt my flowers; but gently spend
Your hony drops: presse not to smell them here:
When they are ripe, their odour will ascend,
And at your lodging with their thanks appeare.

How harsh are thorns to pears! and yet they make
A better hedge, and need lesse reparation.
How smooth are silks compared with a stake,
Or with a stone! yet make no good foundation.

Sometimes thou dost divide thy gifts to man,
Sometimes unite. The Indian nut alone
Is clothing, meat and trencher, drink and can,
Boat, cable, sail and needle, all in one.

Most herbs that grow in brooks, are hot and dry.
Cold fruits warm kernells help against the winde.
The lemmons juice and rind cure mutually.
The whey of milk doth loose, the milk doth binde.

Thy creatures leap not, but expresse a feast,
Where all the guests sit close, and nothing wants.
Frogs marry fish and flesh; bats, bird and beast;
Sponges, non-sense and sense; mines, th' earth & plants.

To show thou art not bound, as if thy lot
Were worse then ours, sometimes thou shiftest hands.
Most things move th' under-jaw; the Crocodile not.
Most things sleep lying; th' Elephant leans or stands.

But who hath praise enough? nay, who hath any?
None can expresse thy works, but he that knows them:
And none can know thy works, which are so many,
And so complete, but onely he that owes them.

All things that are, though they have sev'rall wayes,
Yet in their being joyn with one advise
To honour thee: and so I give thee praise
In all my other hymnes, but in this twice.

Each thing that is, although in use and name
It go for one, hath many wayes in store
To honour thee; and so each hymne thy fame
Extolleth many wayes, yet this one more.

Hope

I gave to Hope a watch of mine: but he
An anchor gave to me.
Then an old prayer-book I did present:
And he an optick sent.
With that I gave a viall full of tears:
But he a few green eares.
Ah Loyterer! I'le no more, no more I'le bring:
I did expect a ring.

Sinnes round

Sorrie I am, my God, sorrie I am,
That my offences course it in a ring.
My thoughts are working like a busie flame,
Untill their cockatrice they hatch and bring:
And when they once have perfected their draughts,
My words take fire from my inflamed thoughts.

My words take fire from my inflamed thoughts,
Which spit it forth like the Sicilian Hill.

They vent the wares, and passe them with their faults,
And by their breathing ventilate the ill.
But words suffice not, where are lewd intentions:
My hands do joyn to finish the inventions.

My hands do joyn to finish the inventions:
And so my sinnes ascend three stories high,
As Babel grew, before there were dissensions.
Yet ill deeds loyter not: for they supplie
New thoughts of sinning: wherefore, to my shame,
Sorrie I am, my God, sorrie I am.

Time

Meeting with Time, Slack thing, said I,
Thy sithe is dull; whet it for shame.
No marvell Sir, he did replie,
If it at length deserve some blame:
  But where one man would have me grinde it,
  Twentie for one too sharp do finde it.

Perhaps some such of old did passe,
Who above all things lov'd this life;
To whom thy sithe a hatchet was,
Which now is but a pruning-knife.
  Christs coming hath made man thy debter,
  Since by thy cutting he grows better.

And in his blessing thou art blest:
For where thou onely wert before
An executioner at best;
Thou art a gard'ner now, and more,
  An usher to convey our souls
  Beyond the utmost starres and poles.

And this is that makes life so long,
While it detains us from our God.
Ev'n pleasures here increase the wrong,
And length of dayes lengthen the rod.
  Who wants the place, where God doth dwell,
  Partakes already half of hell.

Of what strange length must that needs be,
Which ev'n eternitie excludes!
Thus farre Time heard me patiently:
Then chafing said, This man deludes:
  What do I here before his doore?
  He doth not crave lesse time, but more.

Gratefulnesse

Thou that hast giv'n so much to me,
Give one thing more, a grateful heart.
See how thy beggar works on thee
                    By art.

He makes thy gifts occasion more,
And sayes, If he in this be crost,
All thou hast giv'n him heretofore
                    Is lost.

But thou didst reckon, when at first
Thy word our hearts and hands did crave,
What it would come to at the worst
                    To save.

Perpetuall knockings at thy doore,
Tears sullying thy transparent rooms,

Gift upon gift, much would have more,
And comes.

This notwithstanding, thou wentst on,
And didst allow us all our noise:
Nay, thou hast made a sigh and grone
Thy joyes.

Not that thou hast not still above
Much better tunes, then grones can make;
But that these countrey-aires thy love
Did take.

Wherefore I crie, and crie again;
And in no quiet canst thou be,
Till I a thankful heart obtain
Of thee:

Not thankfull, when it pleaseth me;
As if thy blessings had spare dayes:
But such a heart, whose pulse may be
Thy praise.

Peace

Sweet Peace, where dost thou dwell? I humbly crave,
Let me once know.
I sought thee in a secret cave,
And ask'd, if Peace were there.
A hollow winde did seem to answer, No:
Go seek elsewhere.

I did; and going did a rainbow note:

Surely, thought I,
This is the lace of Peaces coat:
I will search out the matter.
But while I lookt, the clouds immediately
Did break and scatter.

Then went I to a garden, and did spy
A gallant flower,
The Crown Imperiall: Sure, said I,
Peace at the root must dwell.
But when I digg'd, I saw a worm devoure
What show'd so well.

At length I met a rev'rend good old man,
Whom when for Peace
I did demand, he thus began:
There was a Prince of old
At Salem dwelt, who liv'd with good increase
Of flock and fold.

He sweetly liv'd; yet sweetnesse did not save
His life from foes.
But after death out of his grave
There sprang twelve stalks of wheat:
Which many wondring at, got some of those
To plant and set.

It prosper'd strangely, and did soon disperse
Through all the earth:
For they that taste it do rehearse,
That vertue lies therein,
A secret vertue bringing peace and mirth
By flight of sinne.

Take of this grain, which in my garden grows,
And grows for you;
Make bread of it: and that repose
And peace, which ev'ry where
With so much earnestnesse you do pursue,
Is onely there.

Confession

O what a cunning guest
Is this same grief! within my heart I made
Closets; and in them many a chest;
And, like a master in my trade,
In those chests, boxes; in each box, a till:
Yet grief knows all, and enters when he will.

No scrue, no piercer can
Into a piece of timber work and winde,
As Gods afflictions into man,
When he a torture hath design'd.
They are too subtill for the subt'llest hearts;
And fall, like rheumes, upon the tendrest parts.

We are the earth; and they,
Like moles within us, heave, and cast about:
And till they foot and clutch their prey,
They never cool, much lesse give out.
No smith can make such locks but they have keyes:
Closets are halls to them; and hearts, high-wayes.

Onely an open breast
Doth shut them out, so that they cannot enter;

Or, if they enter, cannot rest,
But quickly seek some new adventure.
Smooth open hearts no fastning have; but fiction
Doth give a hold and handle to affliction.

Wherefore my faults and sinnes,
Lord, I acknowledge; take thy plagues away:
For since confession pardon winnes,
I challenge here the brightest day,
The clearest diamond: let them do their best,
They shall be thick and cloudie to my breast.

Giddinesse

Oh, what a thing is man! how farre from power,
From setled peace and rest!
He is some twentie sev'rall men at least
Each sev'rall houre.

One while he counts of heav'n, as of his treasure:
But then a thought creeps in,
And calls him coward, who for fear of sinne
Will lose a pleasure.

Now he will fight it out, and to the warres;
Now eat his bread in peace,
And snudge in quiet: now he scorns increase;
Now all day spares.

He builds a house, which quickly down must go,
As if a whirlwinde blew
And crusht the building: and it's partly true,
His minde is so.

O what a sight were Man, if his attires
Did alter with his minde;
And like a Dolphins skinne, his clothes combin'd
With his desires!

Surely if each one saw anothers heart,
There would be no commerce,
No sale or bargain passe: all would disperse,
And live apart.

Lord, mend or rather make us: one creation
Will not suffice our turn:
Except thou make us dayly, we shall spurn
Our own salvation.

Love unknown

Deare Friend, sit down, the tale is long and sad:
And in my faintings I presume your love
Will more complie then help. A Lord I had,
And have, of whom some grounds, which may improve,
I hold for two lives, and both lives in me.
To him I brought a dish of fruit one day,
And in the middle plac'd my heart. But he
(I sigh to say)
Lookt on a servant, who did know his eye
Better then you know me, or (which is one)
Then I my self. The servant instantly
Quitting the fruit, seiz'd on my heart alone,
And threw it in a font, wherein did fall
A stream of bloud, which issu'd from the side
Of a great rock: I well remember all,
And have good cause: there it was dipt and dy'd,

And washt, and wrung: the very wringing yet
Enforceth tears. *Your heart was foul, I fear.*
Indeed 'tis true. I did and do commit
Many a fault more then my lease will bear;
Yet still askt pardon, and was not deni'd.
But you shall heare. After my heart was well,
And clean and fair, as I one even-tide
(I sigh to tell)
Walkt by my self abroad, I saw a large
And spacious fornace flaming, and thereon
A boyling caldron, round about whose verge
Was in great letters set *AFFLICTION.*
The greatnesse shew'd the owner. So I went
To fetch a sacrifice out of my fold,
Thinking with that, which I did thus present,
To warm his love, which I did fear grew cold.
But as my heart did tender it, the man,
Who was to take it from me, slipt his hand,
And threw my heart into the scalding pan;
My heart, that brought it (do you understand?)
The offerers heart. *Your heart was hard, I fear.*
Indeed it's true. I found a callous matter
Began to spread and to expatiate there:
But with a richer drug then scalding water
I bath'd it often, ev'n with holy bloud,
Which at a board, while many drunk bare wine,
A friend did steal into my cup for good,
Ev'n taken inwardly, and most divine
To supple hardnesses. But at the length
Out of the caldron getting, soon I fled
Unto my house, where to repair the strength
Which I had lost, I hasted to my bed.
But when I thought to sleep out all these faults
(I sigh to speak)

I found that some had stuff'd the bed with thoughts,
I would say *thorns*. Deare, could my heart not break,
When with my pleasures ev'n my rest was gone?
Full well I understood, who had been there:
For I had giv'n the key to none, but one:
It must be he. *Your heart was dull, I fear.*
Indeed a slack and sleepie state of minde
Did oft possesse me, so that when I pray'd,
Though my lips went, my heart did stay behinde.
But all my scores were by another paid,
Who took the debt upon him. *Truly, Friend,*
For ought I heare, your Master shows to you
More favour then you wot of. Mark the end.
The Font did onely, what was old, renew:
The Caldron suppled, what was grown too hard:
The Thorns did quicken, what was grown too dull:
All did but strive to mend, what you had marr'd.
Wherefore be cheer'd, and praise him to the full
Each day, each houre, each moment of the week,
Who fain would have you be new, tender, quick.

Mans medley

Heark, how the birds do sing,
And woods do ring.
All creatures have their joy: and man hath his.
Yet if we rightly measure,
Mans joy and pleasure
Rather hereafter, then in present, is.

To this life things of sense
Make their pretence:
In th' other Angels have a right by birth:

Man ties them both alone,
    And makes them one,
With th' one hand touching heav'n, with th' other earth.

In soul he mounts and flies,
    In flesh he dies.
He wears a stuffe whose thread is course and round,
But trimm'd with curious lace,
    And should take place
After the trimming, not the stuffe and ground.

Not that he may not here
    Taste of the cheer,
But as birds drink, and straight lift up their head,
So he must sip and think
    Of better drink
He may attain to, after he is dead.

But as his joyes are double;
    So is his trouble.
He hath two winters, other things but one:
Both frosts and thoughts do nip,
    And bite his lip;
And he of all things fears two deaths alone.

Yet ev'n the greatest griefs
    May be reliefs,
Could he but take them right, and in their wayes.
Happie is he, whose heart
    Hath found the art
To turn his double pains to double praise.

The Storm

If as the windes and waters here below
Do flie and flow,
My sighs and tears as busie were above;
Sure they would move
And much affect thee, as tempestuous times
Amaze poore mortals, and object their crimes.

Starres have their storms, ev'n in a high degree,
As well as we.
A throbbing conscience spurred by remorse
Hath a strange force:
It quits the earth, and mounting more and more
Dares to assault thee, and besiege thy doore.

There it stands knocking, to thy musicks wrong,
And drowns the song.
Glorie and honour are set by, till it
An answer get.
Poets have wrong'd poore storms: such dayes are best;
They purge the aire without, within the breast.

Paradise

I blesse thee, Lord, because I GROW
Among thy trees, which in a ROW
To thee both fruit and order OW.

What open force, or hidden CHARM
Can blast my fruit, or bring me HARM,
While the inclosure is thine ARM?

Inclose me still for fear I START.
Be to me rather sharp and TART,
Then let me want thy hand & ART.

When thou dost greater judgements SPARE,
And with thy knife but prune and PARE,
Ev'n fruitfull trees more fruitfull ARE.

Such sharpnes shows the sweetest FREND:
Such cuttings rather heal then REND:
And such beginnings touch their END.

Divinitie

As men, for fear the starres should sleep and nod,
And trip at night, have spheres suppli'd;
As if a starre were duller then a clod,
Which knows his way without a guide:

Just so the other heav'n they also serve,
Divinities transcendent skie:
Which with the edge of wit they cut and carve.
Reason triumphs, and faith lies by.

Could not that Wisdome, which first broacht the wine,
Have thicken'd it with definitions?
And jagg'd his seamlesse coat, had that been fine,
With curious questions and divisions?

But all the doctrine, which he taught and gave,
Was cleare as heav'n, from whence it came.
At least those beams of truth, which onely save,
Surpasse in brightnesse any flame.

Love God, and love your neighbour. Watch and pray.
Do as ye would be done unto.
O dark instructions; ev'n as dark as day!
Who can these Gordian knots undo?

But he doth bid us take his bloud for wine.
Bid what he please; yet I am sure,
To take and taste what he doth there designe,
Is all that saves, and not obscure.

Then burn thy Epicycles, foolish man;
Break all thy spheres, and save thy head.
Faith needs no staffe of flesh, but stoutly can
To heav'n alone both go, and leade.

Ephes. 4. 30

GRIEVE NOT THE HOLY SPIRIT, &C.

And art thou grieved, sweet and sacred Dove,
When I am sowre,
And crosse thy love?
Grieved for me? the God of strength and power
Griev'd for a worm, which when I tread,
I passe away and leave it dead?

Then weep mine eyes, the God of love doth grieve:
Weep foolish heart,
And weeping live:
For death is drie as dust. Yet if ye part,
End as the night, whose sable hue
Your sinnes expresse; melt into dew.

When sawcie mirth shall knock or call at doore,
Cry out, Get hence,
Or cry no more.
Almightie God doth grieve, he puts on sense:
I sinne not to my grief alone,
But to my Gods too; he doth grone.

Oh take thy lute, and tune it to a strain,
Which may with thee
All day complain.
There can no discord but in ceasing be.
Marbles can weep; and surely strings
More bowels have, then such hard things.

Lord, I adjudge my self to tears and grief,
Ev'n endlesse tears
Without relief.
If a cleare spring for me no time forbears,
But runnes, although I be not drie;
I am no Crystall, what shall I?

Yet if I wail not still, since still to wail
Nature denies;
And flesh would fail,
If my deserts were masters of mine eyes:
Lord, pardon, for thy Sonne makes good
My want of tears with store of bloud.

The Familie

What doth this noise of thoughts within my heart,
As if they had a part?
What do these loud complaints and puling fears,
As if there were no rule or eares?

But, Lord, the house and familie are thine,
Though some of them repine.
Turn out these wranglers, which defile thy seat:
For where thou dwellest all is neat.

First Peace and Silence all disputes controll,
Then Order plaies the soul;
And giving all things their set forms and houres,
Makes of wilde woods sweet walks and bowres.

Humble Obedience neare the doore doth stand,
Expecting a command:
Then whom in waiting nothing seems more slow,
Nothing more quick when she doth go.

Joyes oft are there, and griefs as oft as joyes;
But griefs without a noise:
Yet speak they louder then distemper'd fears.
What is so shrill as silent tears?

This is thy house, with these it doth abound:
And where these are not found,
Perhaps thou com'st sometimes, and for a day;
But not to make a constant stay.

The Size

Content thee, greedie heart.
Modest and moderate joyes to those, that have
Title to more hereafter when they part,
Are passing brave.
Let th' upper springs into the low
Descend and fall, and thou dost flow.

What though some have a fraught
Of cloves and nutmegs, and in cinamon sail;
If thou hast wherewithall to spice a draught,
When griefs prevail;
And for the future time art heir
To th' Isle of spices, is't not fair?

To be in both worlds full
Is more then God was, who was hungrie here.
Wouldst thou his laws of fasting disanull?
Enact good cheer?
Lay out thy joy, yet hope to save it?
Woulds't thou both eat thy cake, and have it?

Great joyes are all at once;
But little do reserve themselves for more:
Those have their hopes; these what they have renounce,
And live on score:
Those are at home; these journey still,
And meet the rest on Sions hill.

Thy Saviour sentenc'd joy,
And in the flesh condemn'd it as unfit,
At least in lump: for such doth oft destroy;
Whereas a bit
Doth tice us on to hopes of more,
And for the present health restore.

A Christians state and case
Is not a corpulent, but a thinne and spare,
Yet active strength: whose long and bonie face
Content and care
Do seem to equally divide,
Like a pretender, not a bride.

Wherefore sit down, good heart;
Grasp not at much, for fear thou losest all.
If comforts fell according to desert,
They would great frosts and snows destroy:
For we should count, Since the last joy.

Then close again the seam,
Which thou hast open'd: do not spread thy robe
In hope of great things. Call to minde thy dream,
An earthly globe,
On whose meridian was engraven,
These seas are tears, and heav'n the haven.

Artillerie

As I one ev'ning sat before my cell,
Me thoughts a starre did shoot into my lap.
I rose, and shook my clothes, as knowing well,
That from small fires comes oft no small mishap.
When suddenly I heard one say,
Do as thou usest, disobey,
Expell good motions from thy breast,
Which have the face of fire, but end in rest.

I, who had heard of musick in the spheres,
But not of speech in starres, began to muse:
But turning to my God, whose ministers
The starres and all things are; If I refuse,
Dread Lord, said I, so oft my good;
Then I refuse not ev'n with bloud
To wash away my stubborn thought:
For I will do or suffer what I ought.

But I have also starres and shooters too,
Born where thy servants both artilleries use.
My tears and prayers night and day do wooe,
And work up to thee; yet thou dost refuse.
Not but I am (I must say still)
Much more oblig'd to do thy will,
Then thou to grant mine: but because
Thy promise now hath ev'n set thee thy laws.

Then we are shooters both, and thou dost deigne
To enter combate with us, and contest
With thine own clay. But I would parley fain:
Shunne not my arrows, and behold my breast.
Yet if thou shunnest, I am thine:
I must be so, if I am mine.
There is no articling with thee:
I am but finite, yet thine infinitely.

Church-rents and schismes

Brave rose, (alas!) where art thou? in the chair
Where thou didst lately so triumph and shine
A worm doth sit, whose many feet and hair
Are the more foul, the more thou wert divine.
This, this hath done it, this did bite the root
And bottome of the leaves: which when the winde
Did once perceive, it blew them under foot,
Where rude unhallow'd steps do crush and grinde
Their beauteous glories. Onely shreds of thee,
And those all bitten, in thy chair I see.

Why doth my Mother blush? is she the rose,
And shows it so? Indeed Christs precious bloud

Gave you a colour once; which when your foes
Thought to let out, the bleeding did you good,
And made you look much fresher then before.
But when debates and fretting jealousies
Did worm and work within you more and more,
Your colour vaded, and calamities
    Turned your ruddie into pale and bleak:
    Your health and beautie both began to break.

Then did your sev'rall parts unloose and start:
Which when your neighbours saw, like a north-winde
They rushed in, and cast them in the dirt
Where Pagans tread. O Mother deare and kinde,
Where shall I get me eyes enough to weep,
As many eyes as starres? since it is night,
And much of Asia and Europe fast asleep,
And ev'n all Africk; would at least I might
    With these two poore ones lick up all the dew,
    Which falls by night, and poure it out for you!

Justice [II]

O dreadfull Justice, what a fright and terrour
            Wast thou of old,
            When sinne and errour
        Did show and shape thy looks to me,
        And through their glasse discolour thee!
He that did but look up, was proud and bold.

The dishes of thy ballance seem'd to gape,
            Like two great pits;
            The beam and scape
        Did like some torturing engine show;

Thy hand above did burn and glow,
Danting the stoutest hearts, the proudest wits.

But now that Christs pure vail presents the sight,
I see no fears:
Thy hand is white,
Thy scales like buckets, which attend
And interchangeably descend,
Lifting to heaven from this well of tears.

For where before thou still didst call on me,
Now I still touch
And harp on thee.
Gods promises have made thee mine;
Why should I justice now decline?
Against me there is none, but for me much.

The Pilgrimage

I travell'd on, seeing the hill, where lay
My expectation.
A long it was and weary way.
The gloomy cave of Desperation
I left on th' one, and on the other side
The rock of Pride.

And so I came to Fancies medow strow'd
With many a flower:
Fain would I here have made abode,
But I was quicken'd by my houre.
So to Cares cops I came, and there got through
With much ado.

That led me to the wilde of Passion, which
Some call the wold;
A wasted place, but sometimes rich.
Here I was robb'd of all my gold,
Save one good Angell, which a friend had ti'd
Close to my side.

At length I got unto the gladsome hill,
Where lay my hope,
Where lay my heart; and climbing still,
When I had gain'd the brow and top,
A lake of brackish waters on the ground
Was all I found.

With that abash'd and struck with many a sting
Of swarming fears,
I fell, and cry'd, Alas my King!
Can both the way and end be tears?
Yet taking heart I rose, and then perceiv'd
I was deceiv'd:

My hill was further: so I flung away,
Yet heard a crie
Just as I went, *None goes that way*
And lives: If that be all, said I,
After so foul a journey death is fair,
And but a chair.

Complaining

Do not beguile my heart,
Because thou art
My power and wisdome. Put me not to shame,

Because I am
Thy clay that weeps, thy dust that calls.

Thou art the Lord of glorie;
The deed and storie
Are both thy due: but I a silly flie,
That live or die
According as the weather falls.

Art thou all justice, Lord?
Shows not thy word
More attributes? Am I all throat or eye,
To weep or crie?
Have I no parts but those of grief?

Let not thy wrathfull power
Afflict my houre,
My inch of life: or let thy gracious power
Contract my houre,
That I may climbe and finde relief.

The Discharge

Busie enquiring heart, what wouldst thou know?
Why dost thou prie,
And turn, and leer, and with a licorous eye
Look high and low;
And in thy lookings stretch and grow?

Hast thou not made thy counts, and summ'd up all?
Did not thy heart
Give up the whole, and with the whole depart?
Let what will fall:
That which is past who can recall?

Thy life is Gods, thy time to come is gone,
And is his right.
He is thy night at noon: he is at night
Thy noon alone.
The crop is his, for he hath sown.

And well it was for thee, when this befell,
That God did make
Thy businesse his, and in thy life partake:
For thou canst tell,
If it be his once, all is well.

Onely the present is thy part and fee.
And happy thou,
If, though thou didst not beat thy future brow,
Thou couldst well see
What present things requir'd of thee.

They ask enough; why shouldst thou further go?
Raise not the mudde
Of future depths, but drink the cleare and good.
Dig not for wo
In times to come; for it will grow.

Man and the present fit: if he provide,
He breaks the square.
This houre is mine: if for the next I care,
I grow too wide,
And do encroach upon deaths side.

For death each houre environs and surrounds.
He that would know
And care for future chances, cannot go
Unto those grounds,
But through a Church-yard which them bounds.

Things present shrink and die: but they that spend
Their thoughts and sense
On future grief, do not remove it thence,
But it extend,
And draw the bottome out an end.

God chains the dog till night: wilt loose the chain,
And wake thy sorrow?
Wilt thou forestall it, and now grieve to morrow,
And then again
Grieve over freshly all thy pain?

Either grief will not come: or if it must,
Do not forecast.
And while it cometh, it is almost past.
Away distrust:
My God hath promis'd; he is just.

Praise [II]

King of Glorie, King of Peace,
I will love thee:
And that love may never cease,
I will move thee.

Thou hast granted my request,
Thou hast heard me:
Thou didst note my working breast,
Thou hast spar'd me.

Wherefore with my utmost art
I will sing thee,
And the cream of all my heart
I will bring thee.

Though my sinnes against me cried,
Thou didst cleare me;
And alone, when they replied,
Thou didst heare me.

Sev'n whole dayes, not one in seven,
I will praise thee.
In my heart, though not in heaven,
I can raise thee.

Thou grew'st soft and moist with tears,
Thou relentedst:
And when Justice call'd for fears,
Thou dissentedst.

Small it is, in this poore sort
To enroll thee:
Ev'n eternitie is too short
To extoll thee.

The Bag

Away despair! my gracious Lord doth heare.
Though windes and waves assault my keel,
He doth preserve it: he doth steer,
Ev'n when the boat seems most to reel.
Storms are the triumph of his art:
Well may he close his eyes, but not his heart.

Hast thou not heard, that my Lord JESUS di'd?
Then let me tell thee a strange storie.
The God of power, as he did ride
In his majestick robes of glorie,

Resolv'd to light; and so one day
He did descend, undressing all the way.

The starres his tire of light and rings obtain'd,
The cloud his bow, the fire his spear,
The sky his azure mantle gain'd.
And when they ask'd, what he would wear;
He smil'd and said as he did go,
He had new clothes a making here below.

When he was come, as travellers are wont,
He did repair unto an inne.
Both then, and after, many a brunt
He did endure to cancell sinne:
And having giv'n the rest before,
Here he gave up his life to pay our score.

But as he was returning, there came one
That ran upon him with a spear.
He, who came hither all alone,
Bringing nor man, nor arms, nor fear,
Receiv'd the blow upon his side,
And straight he turn'd, and to his brethren cry'd,

If ye have any thing to send or write,
I have no bag, but here is room:
Unto my Fathers hands and sight,
Beleeve me, it shall safely come.
That I shall minde, what you impart,
Look, you may put it very neare my heart.

Or if hereafter any of my friends
Will use me in this kinde, the doore
Shall still be open; what he sends

I will present, and somewhat more,
Not to his hurt. Sighs will convey
Any thing to me. Harke, Despair away.

The Jews

Poore nation, whose sweet sap and juice
Our cyens have purloin'd, and left you drie:
Whose streams we got by the Apostles sluce,
And use in baptisme, while ye pine and die:
Who by not keeping once, became a debter;
And now by keeping lose the letter:

Oh that my prayers! mine, alas!
Oh that some Angel might a trumpet sound;
At which the Church falling upon her face
Should crie so loud, untill the trump were drown'd,
And by that crie of her deare Lord obtain,
That your sweet sap might come again!

The Collar

I struck the board, and cry'd, No more.
I will abroad.
What? shall I ever sigh and pine?
My lines and life are free; free as the rode,
Loose as the winde, as large as store.
Shall I be still in suit?
Have I no harvest but a thorn
To let me bloud, and not restore
What I have lost with cordiall fruit?
Sure there was wine

Before my sighs did drie it: there was corn
Before my tears did drown it.
Is the yeare onely lost to me?
Have I no bayes to crown it?
No flowers, no garlands gay? all blasted?
All wasted?
Not so, my heart: but there is fruit,
And thou hast hands.
Recover all thy sigh-blown age
On double pleasures: leave thy cold dispute
Of what is fit, and not. Forsake thy cage,
Thy rope of sands,
Which pettie thoughts have made, and made to thee
Good cable, to enforce and draw,
And be thy law,
While thou didst wink and wouldst not see.
Away; take heed:
I will abroad.
Call in thy deaths head there: tie up thy fears.
He that forbears
To suit and serve his need,
Deserves his load.
But as I rav'd and grew more fierce and wilde
At every word,
Me thoughts I heard one calling, *Child!*
And I reply'd, *My Lord.*

The Glimpse

Whither away delight?
Thou cam'st but now; wilt thou so soon depart,
And give me up to night?
For many weeks of lingring pain and smart
But one half houre of comfort to my heart?

Me thinks delight should have
More skill in musick, and keep better time.
Wert thou a winde or wave,
They quickly go and come with lesser crime:
Flowers look about, and die not in their prime.

Thy short abode and stay
Feeds not, but addes to the desire of meat.
Lime begg'd of old, they say,
A neighbour spring to cool his inward heat;
Which by the springs accesse grew much more great.

In hope of thee my heart
Pickt here and there a crumme, and would not die;
But constant to his part,
When as my fears foretold this, did replie,
A slender thread a gentle guest will tie.

Yet if the heart that wept
Must let thee go, return when it doth knock.
Although thy heap be kept
For future times, the droppings of the stock
May oft break forth, and never break the lock.

If I have more to spinne,
The wheel shall go, so that thy stay be short.
Thou knowst how grief and sinne
Disturb the work. O make me not their sport,
Who by thy coming may be made a court!

Clasping of hands

Lord, thou art mine, and I am thine,
If mine I am: and thine much more,

Then I or ought, or can be mine.
Yet to be thine, doth me restore;
So that again I now am mine,
And with advantage mine the more,
Since this being mine, brings with it thine,
And thou with me dost thee restore.
    If I without thee would be mine,
    I neither should be mine nor thine.

Lord, I am thine, and thou art mine:
So mine thou art, that something more
I may presume thee mine, then thine.
For thou didst suffer to restore
Not thee, but me, and to be mine,
And with advantage mine the more,
Since thou in death wast none of thine,
Yet then as mine didst me restore.
    O be mine still! still make me thine!
    Or rather make no Thine and Mine!

Praise [III]

    Lord, I will mean and speak thy praise,
            Thy praise alone.
My busie heart shall spin it all my dayes:
    And when it stops for want of store,
Then will I wring it with a sigh or grone,
        That thou mayst yet have more.

    When thou dost favour any action,
            It runnes, it flies:
All things concurre to give it a perfection.
    That which had but two legs before,

When thou dost blesse, hath twelve: one wheel doth rise
To twentie then, or more.

But when thou dost on businesse blow,
It hangs, it clogs:
Not all the teams of Albion in a row
Can hale or draw it out of doore.
Legs are but stumps, and Pharaohs wheels but logs,
And struggling hinders more.

Thousands of things do thee employ
In ruling all
This spacious globe: Angels must have their joy,
Devils their rod, the sea his shore,
The windes their stint: and yet when I did call,
Thou heardst my call, and more.

I have not lost one single tear:
But when mine eyes
Did weep to heav'n, they found a bottle there
(As we have boxes for the poore)
Readie to take them in; yet of a size
That would contain much more.

But after thou hadst slipt a drop
From thy right eye,
(Which there did hang like streamers neare the top
Of some fair church, to show the sore
And bloudie battell which thou once didst trie)
The glasse was full and more.

Wherefore I sing. Yet since my heart,
Though press'd, runnes thin;
O that I might some other hearts convert,

And so take up at use good store:
That to thy chest there might be coming in
Both all my praise, and more!

Josephs coat

Wounded I sing, tormented I indite,
Thrown down I fall into a bed, and rest:
Sorrow hath chang'd its note: such is his will,
Who changeth all things, as him pleaseth best.
For well he knows, if but one grief and smart
Among my many had his full career,
Sure it would carrie with it ev'n my heart,
And both would runne untill they found a biere
To fetch the bodie; both being due to grief.
But he hath spoil'd the race; and giv'n to anguish
One of Joyes coats, ticing it with relief
To linger in me, and together languish.
I live to shew his power, who once did bring
My *joyes* to *weep,* and now my *griefs* to *sing.*

The Pulley

When God at first made man,
Having a glasse of blessings standing by;
Let us (said he) poure on him all we can:
Let the worlds riches, which dispersed lie,
Contract into a span.

So strength first made a way;
Then beautie flow'd, then wisdome, honour, pleasure:
When almost all was out, God made a stay,

Perceiving that alone of all his treasure
Rest in the bottome lay.

For if I should (said he)
Bestow this jewell also on my creature,
He would adore my gifts in stead of me,
And rest in Nature, not the God of Nature:
So both should losers be.

Yet let him keep the rest,
But keep them with repining restlesnesse:
Let him be rich and wearie, that at least,
If goodnesse leade him not, yet wearinesse
May tosse him to my breast.

The Priesthood

Blest Order, which in power dost so excell,
That with th' one hand thou liftest to the sky,
And with the other throwest down to hell
In thy just censures; fain would I draw nigh,
Fain put thee on, exchanging my lay-sword
For that of th' holy Word.

But thou art fire, sacred and hallow'd fire;
And I but earth and clay: should I presume
To wear thy habit, the severe attire
My slender compositions might consume.
I am both foul and brittle; much unfit
To deal in holy Writ.

Yet have I often seen, by cunning hand
And force of fire, what curious things are made

Of wretched earth. Where once I scorn'd to stand,
That earth is fitted by the fire and trade
Of skilfull artists, for the boards of those
Who make the bravest shows.

But since those great ones, be they ne're so great,
Come from the earth, from whence those vessels come;
So that at once both feeder, dish, and meat
Have one beginning and one finall summe:
I do not greatly wonder at the sight,
If earth in earth delight.

But th' holy men of God such vessels are,
As serve him up, who all the world commands:
When God vouchsafeth to become our fare,
Their hands convey him, who conveys their hands.
O what pure things, most pure must those things be,
Who bring my God to me!

Wherefore I dare not, I, put forth my hand
To hold the Ark, although it seem to shake
Through th' old sinnes and new doctrines of our land.
Onely, since God doth often vessels make
Of lowly matter for high uses meet,
I throw me at his feet.

There will I lie, untill my Maker seek
For some mean stuffe whereon to show his skill:
Then is my time. The distance of the meek
Doth flatter power. Lest good come short of ill
In praising might, the poore do by submission
What pride by opposition.

The Search

Whither, O, whither art thou fled,
My Lord, my Love?
My searches are my daily bread;
Yet never prove.

My knees pierce th' earth, mine eies the skie;
And yet the sphere
And centre both to me denie
That thou art there.

Yet can I mark how herbs below
Grow green and gay,
As if to meet thee they did know,
While I decay.

Yet can I mark how starres above
Simper and shine,
As having keyes unto thy love,
While poore I pine.

I sent a sigh to seek thee out,
Deep drawn in pain,
Wing'd like an arrow: but my scout
Returns in vain.

I tun'd another (having store)
Into a grone;
Because the search was dumbe before:
But all was one.

Lord, dost thou some new fabrick mould,
Which favour winnes,

And keeps thee present, leaving th' old
Unto their sinnes?

Where is my God? what hidden place
Conceals thee still?
What covert dare eclipse thy face?
Is it thy will?

O let not that of any thing;
Let rather brasse,
Or steel, or mountains be thy ring,
And I will passe.

Thy will such an intrenching is,
As passeth thought:
To it all strength, all subtilties
Are things of nought.

Thy will such a strange distance is,
As that to it
East and West touch, the poles do kisse,
And parallels meet.

Since then my grief must be as large,
As is thy space,
Thy distance from me; see my charge,
Lord, see my case.

O take these barres, these lengths away;
Turn, and restore me:
Be not Almightie, let me say,
Against, but for me.

When thou dost turn, and wilt be neare;
        What edge so keen,
What point so piercing can appeare
        To come between?

For as thy absence doth excell
        All distance known:
So doth thy nearnesse bear the bell,
        Making two one.

Grief

O who will give me tears? Come all ye springs,
Dwell in my head & eyes: come clouds, & rain:
My grief hath need of all the watry things,
That nature hath produc'd. Let ev'ry vein
Suck up a river to supply mine eyes,
My weary weeping eyes, too drie for me,
Unlesse they get new conduits, new supplies
To bear them out, and with my state agree.
What are two shallow foords, two little spouts
Of a lesse world? the greater is but small,
A narrow cupboard for my griefs and doubts,
Which want provision in the midst of all.
Verses, ye are too fine a thing, too wise
For my rough sorrows: cease, be dumbe and mute,
Give up your feet and running to mine eyes,
And keep your measures for some lovers lute,
Whose grief allows him musick and a ryme:
For mine excludes both measure, tune, and time.
        Alas, my God!

The Crosse

What is this strange and uncouth thing?
To make me sigh, and seek, and faint, and die,
Untill I had some place, where I might sing,
And serve thee; and not onely I,
But all my wealth and familie might combine
To set thy honour up, as our designe.

And then when after much delay,
Much wrastling, many a combate, this deare end,
So much desir'd, is giv'n, to take away
My power to serve thee; to unbend
All my abilities, my designes confound,
And lay my threatnings bleeding on the ground.

One ague dwelleth in my bones,
Another in my soul (the memorie
What I would do for thee; if once my grones
Could be allow'd for harmonie):
I am in all a weak disabled thing,
Save in the sight thereof, where strength doth sting.

Besides, things sort not to my will,
Ev'n when my will doth studie thy renown:
Thou turnest th' edge of all things on me still,
Taking me up to throw me down:
So that, ev'n when my hopes seem to be sped,
I am to grief alive, to them as dead.

To have my aim, and yet to be
Further from it then when I bent my bow;
To make my hopes my torture, and the fee
Of all my woes another wo,

Is in the midst of delicates to need,
And ev'n in Paradise to be a weed.

Ah my deare Father, ease my smart!
These contrarieties crush me: these crosse actions
Doe winde a rope about, and cut my heart:
And yet since these thy contradictions
Are properly a crosse felt by thy Sonne,
With but foure words, my words, *Thy will be done.*

The Flower

How fresh, O Lord, how sweet and clean
Are thy returns! ev'n as the flowers in spring;
To which, besides their own demean,
The late-past frosts tributes of pleasure bring.
Grief melts away
Like snow in May,
As if there were no such cold thing.

Who would have thought my shrivel'd heart
Could have recover'd greennesse? It was gone
Quite under ground; as flowers depart
To see their mother-root, when they have blown;
Where they together
All the hard weather,
Dead to the world, keep house unknown.

These are thy wonders, Lord of power,
Killing and quickning, bringing down to hell
And up to heaven in an houre;
Making a chiming of a passing-bell.
We say amisse,

This or that is:
Thy word is all, if we could spell.

O that I once past changing were,
Fast in thy Paradise, where no flower can wither!
Many a spring I shoot up fair,
Offring at heav'n, growing and groning thither:
Nor doth my flower
Want a spring-showre,
My sinnes and I joining together.

But while I grow in a straight line,
Still upwards bent, as if heav'n were mine own,
Thy anger comes, and I decline:
What frost to that? what pole is not the zone,
Where all things burn,
When thou dost turn,
And the least frown of thine is shown?

And now in age I bud again,
After so many deaths I live and write;
I once more smell the dew and rain,
And relish versing: O my onely light,
It cannot be
That I am he
On whom thy tempests fell all night.

These are thy wonders, Lord of love,
To make us see we are but flowers that glide:
Which when we once can finde and prove,
Thou hast a garden for us, where to bide.
Who would be more,
Swelling through store,
Forfeit their Paradise by their pride.

Dotage

False glozing pleasures, casks of happinesse,
Foolish night-fires, womens and childrens wishes,
Chases in Arras, guilded emptinesse,
Shadows well mounted, dreams in a career,
Embroider'd lyes, nothing between two dishes;
These are the pleasures here.

True earnest sorrows, rooted miseries,
Anguish in grain, vexations ripe and blown,
Sure-footed griefs, solid calamities,
Plain demonstrations, evident and cleare,
Fetching their proofs ev'n from the very bone;
These are the sorrows here.

But oh the folly of distracted men,
Who griefs in earnest, joyes in jest pursue;
Preferring, like brute beasts, a lothsome den
Before a court, ev'n that above so cleare,
Where are no sorrows, but delights more true
Then miseries are here!

The Sonne

Let forrain nations of their language boast,
What fine varietie each tongue affords:
I like our language, as our men and coast:
Who cannot dresse it well, want wit, not words.
How neatly doe we give one onely name
To parents issue and the sunnes bright starre!
A sonne is light and fruit; a fruitfull flame
Chasing the fathers dimnesse, carri'd farre

From the first man in th' East, to fresh and new
Western discov'ries of posteritie.
So in one word our Lords humilitie
We turn upon him in a sense most true:
    For what Christ once in humblenesse began,
    We him in glorie call, *The Sonne of Man.*

A true Hymne

            My joy, my life, my crown!
        My heart was meaning all the day,
            Somewhat it fain would say:
And still it runneth mutt'ring up and down
With onely this, *My joy, my life, my crown.*

            Yet slight not these few words:
        If truly said, they may take part
            Among the best in art.
The finenesse which a hymne or psalme affords,
Is, when the soul unto the lines accords.

            He who craves all the minde,
        And all the soul, and strength, and time,
            If the words onely ryme,
Justly complains, that somewhat is behinde
To make his verse, or write a hymne in kinde.

            Whereas if th' heart be moved,
        Although the verse be somewhat scant,
            God doth supplie the want.
As when th' heart sayes (sighing to be approved)
O, could I love! and stops: God writeth, *Loved.*

The Answer

My comforts drop and melt away like snow:
I shake my head, and all the thoughts and ends,
Which my fierce youth did bandie, fall and flow
Like leaves about me: or like summer friends,
Flyes of estates and sunne-shine. But to all,
Who think me eager, hot, and undertaking,
But in my prosecutions slack and small;
As a young exhalation, newly waking,
Scorns his first bed of dirt, and means the sky;
But cooling by the way, grows pursie and slow,
And setling to a cloud, doth live and die
In that dark state of tears: to all, that so
    Show me, and set me, I have one reply,
    Which they that know the rest, know more then I.

A Dialogue-Antheme

CHRISTIAN. DEATH.

Chr. Alas, poore Death, where is thy glorie?
    Where is thy famous force, thy ancient sting?
Dea. *Alas poore mortall, void of storie,*
    Go spell and reade how I have kill'd thy King.
Chr. Poore Death! and who was hurt thereby?
    Thy curse being laid on him, makes thee accurst.
Dea. *Let losers talk: yet thou shalt die;*
    These arms shall crush thee.
Chr.   Spare not, do thy worst.
    I shall be one day better then before:
    Thou so much worse, that thou shalt be no more.

Bitter-sweet

Ah my deare angrie Lord,
Since thou dost love, yet strike;
Cast down, yet help afford;
Sure I will do the like.

I will complain, yet praise;
I will bewail, approve:
And all my sowre-sweet dayes
I will lament, and love.

The Glance

When first thy sweet and gracious eye
Vouchsaf'd ev'n in the midst of youth and night
To look upon me, who before did lie
Weltring in sinne;
I felt a sugred strange delight,
Passing all cordials made by any art,
Bedew, embalme, and overrunne my heart,
And take it in.

Since that time many a bitter storm
My soul hath felt, ev'n able to destroy,
Had the malicious and ill-meaning harm
His swing and sway:
But still thy sweet originall joy,
Sprung from thine eye, did work within my soul,
And surging griefs, when they grew bold, controll,
And got the day.

If thy first glance so powerfull be,
A mirth but open'd and seal'd up again;
What wonders shall we feel, when we shall see
Thy full-ey'd love!
When thou shalt look us out of pain,
And one aspect of thine spend in delight
More then a thousand sunnes disburse in light,
In heav'n above.

Marie Magdalene

When blessed Marie wip'd her Saviours feet,
(Whose precepts she had trampled on before)
And wore them for a jewell on her head,
Shewing his steps should be the street,
Wherein she thenceforth evermore
With pensive humblenesse would live and tread:

She being stain'd her self, why did she strive
To make him clean, who could not be defil'd?
Why kept she not her tears for her own faults,
And not his feet? Though we could dive
In tears like seas, our sinnes are pil'd
Deeper then they, in words, and works, and thoughts.

Deare soul, she knew who did vouchsafe and deigne
To bear her filth; and that her sinnes did dash
Ev'n God himself: wherefore she was not loth,
As she had brought wherewith to stain,
So to bring in wherewith to wash:
And yet in washing one, she washed both.

Aaron

Holinesse on the head,
Light and perfections on the breast,
Harmonious bells below, raising the dead
To leade them unto life and rest:
Thus are true Aarons drest.

Profanenesse in my head,
Defects and darknesse in my breast,
A noise of passions ringing me for dead
Unto a place where is no rest:
Poore priest thus am I drest.

Onely another head
I have, another heart and breast,
Another musick, making live not dead,
Without whom I could have no rest:
In him I am well drest.

Christ is my onely head,
My alone onely heart and breast,
My onely musick, striking me ev'n dead;
That to the old man I may rest,
And be in him new drest.

So holy in my head,
Perfect and light in my deare breast,
My doctrine tun'd by Christ, (who is not dead,
But lives in me while I do rest)
Come people; Aaron's drest.

The Odour. 2 Cor. 2. 15

How sweetly doth *My Master* sound! *My Master!*
As Amber-greese leaves a rich sent
Unto the taster:
So do these words a sweet content,
An orientall fragrancie, *My Master.*

With these all day I do perfume my minde,
My minde ev'n thrust into them both:
That I might finde
What cordials make this curious broth,
This broth of smells, that feeds and fats my minde.

My Master, shall I speak? O that to thee
My servant were a little so,
As flesh may be;
That these two words might creep & grow
To some degree of spicinesse to thee!

Then should the Pomander, which was before
A speaking sweet, mend by reflection,
And tell me more:
For pardon of my imperfection
Would warm and work it sweeter then before.

For when *My Master,* which alone is sweet,
And ev'n in my unworthinesse pleasing,
Shall call and meet,
My servant, as thee not displeasing,
That call is but the breathing of the sweet.

This breathing would with gains by sweetning me
(As sweet things traffick when they meet)
Return to thee.
And so this new commerce and sweet
Should all my life employ and busie me.

The Foil

If we could see below
The sphere of vertue, and each shining grace
As plainly as that above doth show;
This were the better skie, the brighter place.

God hath made starres the foil
To set off vertues; griefs to set off sinning:
Yet in this wretched world we toil,
As if grief were not foul, nor vertue winning.

The Forerunners

The harbingers are come. See, see their mark;
White is their colour, and behold my head.
But must they have my brain? must they dispark
Those sparkling notions, which therein were bred?
Must dulnesse turn me to a clod?
Yet have they left me, *Thou art still my God.*

Good men ye be, to leave me my best room,
Ev'n all my heart, and what is lodged there:
I passe not, I, what of the rest become,
So *Thou art still my God,* be out of fear.
He will be pleased with that dittie;
And if I please him, I write fine and wittie.

Farewell sweet phrases, lovely metaphors.
But will ye leave me thus? when ye before
Of stews and brothels onely knew the doores,
Then did I wash you with my tears, and more,
        Brought you to Church well drest and clad:
My God must have my best, ev'n all I had.

Lovely enchanting language, sugar-cane,
Hony of roses, whither wilt thou flie?
Hath some fond lover tic'd thee to thy bane?
And wilt thou leave the Church, and love a stie?
        Fie, thou wilt soil thy broider'd coat,
And hurt thy self, and him that sings the note.

Let foolish lovers, if they will love dung,
With canvas, not with arras, clothe their shame:
Let follie speak in her own native tongue.
True beautie dwells on high: ours is a flame
        But borrow'd thence to light us thither.
Beautie and beauteous words should go together.

Yet if you go, I passe not; take your way:
For, *Thou art still my God,* is all that ye
Perhaps with more embellishment can say.
Go birds of spring: let winter have his fee;
        Let a bleak palenesse chalk the doore,
So all within be livelier then before.

The Rose

Presse me not to take more pleasure
        In this world of surgred lies,
And to use a larger measure
        Then my strict, yet welcome size.

First, there is no pleasure here:
Colour'd griefs indeed there are,
Blushing woes, that look as cleare
As if they could beautie spare.

Or if such deceits there be,
Such delights I meant to say;
There are no such things to me,
Who have pass'd my right away.

But I will not much oppose
Unto what you now advise:
Onely take this gentle rose,
And therein my answer lies.

What is fairer then a rose?
What is sweeter? yet it purgeth.
Purgings enmitie disclose,
Enmitie forbearance urgeth.

If then all that worldings prize
Be contracted to a rose;
Sweetly there indeed it lies,
But it biteth in the close.

So this flower doth judge and sentence
Worldly joyes to be a scourge:
For they all produce repentance,
And repentance is a purge.

But I health, not physick choose:
Onely though I you oppose,
Say that fairly I refuse,
For my answer is a rose.

Discipline

Throw away thy rod,
Throw away thy wrath:
                    O my God,
Take the gentle path.

For my hearts desire
Unto thine is bent:
                    I aspire
To a full consent.

Not a word or look
I affect to own,
                    But by book,
And thy book alone.

Though I fail, I weep:
Though I halt in pace,
                    Yet I creep
To the throne of grace.

Then let wrath remove;
Love will do the deed:
                    For with love
Stonie hearts will bleed.

Love is swift of foot;
Love's a man of warre,
                    And can shoot,
And can hit from farre.

Who can scape his bow?
That which wrought on thee,

Brought thee low,
Needs must work on me.

Throw away thy rod;
Though man frailties hath,
Thou art God:
Throw away thy wrath.

The Invitation

Come ye hither All, whose taste
Is your waste;
Save your cost, and mend your fare.
God is here prepar'd and drest,
And the feast,
God, in whom all dainties are.

Come ye hither All, whom wine
Doth define,
Naming you not to your good:
Weep what ye have drunk amisse,
And drink this,
Which before ye drink is bloud.

Come ye hither All, whom pain
Doth arraigne,
Bringing all your sinnes to sight:
Taste and fear not: God is here
In this cheer,
And on sinne doth cast the fright.

Come ye hither All, whom joy
Doth destroy,

While ye graze without your bounds:
Here is joy that drowneth quite
Your delight,
As a floud the lower grounds.

Come ye hither All, whose love
Is your dove,
And exalts you to the skie:
Here is love, which having breath
Ev'n in death,
After death can never die.

Lord I have invited all,
And I shall
Still invite, still call to thee:
For it seems but just and right
In my sight,
Where is All, there All should be.

The Banquet

Welcome sweet and sacred cheer,
Welcome deare;
With me, in me, live and dwell:
For thy neatnesse passeth sight,
Thy delight
Passeth tongue to taste or tell.

O what sweetnesse from the bowl
Fills my soul,
Such as is, and makes divine!
Is some starre (fled from the sphere)
Melted there,
As we sugar melt in wine?

Or hath sweetnesse in the bread
                Made a head
To subdue the smell of sinne;
Flowers, and gummes, and powders giving
                All their living,
Lest the Enemy should winne?

Doubtlesse, neither starre nor flower
                Hath the power
Such a sweetnesse to impart:
Onely God, who gives perfumes,
                Flesh assumes,
And with it perfumes my heart.

But as Pomanders and wood
                Still are good,
Yet being bruis'd are better sented:
God, to show how farre his love
                Could improve,
Here, as broken, is presented.

When I had forgot my birth,
                And on earth
In delights of earth was drown'd;
God took bloud, and needs would be
                Spilt with me,
And so found me on the ground.

Having rais'd me to look up,
                In a cup
Sweetly he doth meet my taste.
But I still being low and short,
                Farre from court,
Wine becomes a wing at last.

For with it alone I flie,
To the skie:
Where I wipe mine eyes, and see
What I seek, for what I sue;
Him I view,
Who hath done so much for me.

Let the wonder of his pitie
Be my dittie,
And take up my lines and life:
Hearken under pain of death,
Hands and breath;
Strive in this, and love the strife.

The Posie

Let wits contest,
And with their words and posies windows fill:
Lesse then the least
Of all thy mercies, is my posie still.

This on my ring,
This by my picture, in my book I write:
Whether I sing,
Or say, or dictate, this is my delight.

Invention rest,
Comparisons go play, wit use thy will:
Lesse then the least
Of all Gods mercies, is my posie still.

A Parodie

Souls joy, when thou art gone,
And I alone,
Which cannot be,
Because thou dost abide with me,
And I depend on thee;

Yet when thou dost suppresse
The cheerfulnesse
Of thy abode,
And in my powers not stirre abroad,
But leave me to my load:

O what a damp and shade
Doth me invade!
No stormie night
Can so afflict or so affright,
As thy eclipsed light.

Ah Lord! do not withdraw,
Lest want of aw
Make Sinne appeare;
And when thou dost but shine less cleare,
Say, that thou art not here.

And then what life I have,
While Sinne doth rave,
And falsly boast,
That I may seek, but thou art lost;
Thou and alone thou know'st.

O what a deadly cold
Doth me infold!

I half beleeve,
That Sinne sayes true: but while I grieve,
Thou com'st and dost relieve.

The Elixir

Teach me, my God and King,
In all things thee to see,
And what I do in any thing,
To do it as for thee:

Not rudely, as a beast,
To runne into an action;
But still to make thee prepossest,
And give it his perfection.

A man that looks on glasse,
On it may stay his eye;
Or if he pleaseth, through it passe,
And then the heav'n espie.

All may of thee partake:
Nothing can be so mean,
Which with his tincture (for thy sake)
Will not grow bright and clean.

A servant with this clause
Makes drudgerie divine:
Who sweeps a room, as for thy laws,
Makes that and th' action fine.

This is the famous stone
That turneth all to gold:

For that which God doth touch and own
    Cannot for lesse be told.

A Wreath

A Wreathed garland of deserved praise,
Of praise deserved, unto thee I give,
I give to thee, who knowest all my wayes,
My crooked winding wayes, wherein I live,
Wherein I die, not live: for life is straight,
Straight as a line, and ever tends to thee,
To thee, who art more farre above deceit,
Then deceit seems above simplicitie.
Give me simplicitie, that I may live,
So live and like, that I may know, thy wayes,
Know them and practise them: then shall I give
For this poore wreath, give thee a crown of praise.

Death

Death, thou wast once an uncouth hideous thing,
        Nothing but bones,
    The sad effect of sadder grones:
Thy mouth was open, but thou couldst not sing.

For we consider'd thee as at some six
        Or ten yeares hence,
    After the losse of life and sense,
Flesh being turn'd to dust, and bones to sticks.

We lookt on this side of thee, shooting short;
        Where we did finde

The shells of fledge souls left behinde,
Dry dust, which sheds no tears, but may extort.

But since our Saviours death did put some bloud
Into thy face;
Thou art grown fair and full of grace,
Much in request, much sought for as a good.

For we do now behold thee gay and glad,
As at dooms-day;
When souls shall wear their new aray,
And all thy bones with beautie shall be clad.

Therefore we can go die as sleep, and trust
Half that we have
Unto an honest faithfull grave;
Making our pillows either down, or dust.

Dooms-day

Come away,
Make no delay.
Summon all the dust to rise,
Till it stirre, and rubbe the eyes;
While this member jogs the other,
Each one whispring, *Live you brother?*

Come away,
Make this the day.
Dust, alas, no musick feels,
But thy trumpet: then it kneels,
As peculiar notes and strains
Cure Tarantulas raging pains.

Come away,
O make no stay!
Let the graves make their confession,
Lest at length they plead possession:
Fleshes stubbornnesse may have
Read that lesson to the grave.

Come away,
Thy flock doth stray.
Some to windes their bodie lend,
And in them may drown a friend:
Some in noisome vapours grow
To a plague and publick wo.

Come away,
Help our decay.
Man is out of order hurl'd,
Parcel'd out to all the world.
Lord, thy broken consort raise,
And the musick shall be praise.

Judgement

Almightie Judge, how shall poore wretches brook
Thy dreadfull look,
Able a heart of iron to appall,
When thou shalt call
For ev'ry mans peculiar book?

What others mean to do, I know not well;
Yet I heare tell,
That some will turn thee to some leaves therein
So void of sinne,
That they in merit shall excell.

But I resolve, when thou shalt call for mine,
That to decline,
And thrust a Testament into thy hand:
Let that be scann'd.
There thou shalt finde my faults are thine.

Heaven

O who will show me those delights on high?
Echo. I.
Thou Echo, thou art mortall, all men know.
Echo. No.
Wert thou not born among the trees and leaves?
Echo. Leaves.
And are there any leaves, that still abide?
Echo. Bide.
What leaves are they? impart the matter wholly.
Echo. Holy.
Are holy leaves the Echo then of blisse?
Echo. Yes.
Then tell me, what is that supreme delight?
Echo. Light.
Light to the minde: what shall the will enjoy?
Echo. Joy.
But are there cares and businesse with the pleasure?
Echo. Leisure.
Light, joy, and leisure; but shall they persever?
Echo. Ever.

Love [III]

Love bade me welcome: yet my soul drew back,
Guiltie of dust and sinne.

But quick-ey'd Love, observing me grow slack
From my first entrance in,
Drew nearer to me, sweetly questioning,
If I lack'd any thing.

A guest, I answer'd, worthy to be here:
Love said, You shall be he.
I the unkinde, ungratefull? Ah my deare,
I cannot look on thee.
Love took my hand, and smiling did reply,
Who made the eyes but I?

Truth Lord, but I have marr'd them: let my shame
Go where it doth deserve.
And know you not, sayes Love, who bore the blame?
My deare, then I will serve.
You must sit down, sayes Love, and taste my meat:
So I did sit and eat.

FINIS.

Glory be to God *on high*
And on earth peace
Good will towards men.

About the Text

The Altar

Line 4 Exodus 20:25. **13–14** Luke 19:40.

The Sacrifice

The poem derives from the Improperia, the Reproaches from the Cross, for Good Friday. **Line 1** Lamentations 1:12 and Matthew 27:39. **107** Matthew 27:25. **161–163** Isaiah 5:1–7. **242** Matthew 14:36.

The Thanksgiving

Line 4 *preventest:* anticipates. **5** Luke 22:44, *store:* abundance. **14** *posie:* bouquet. **33** *spittle:* hospital, poorhouse. *common wayes:* public highways. **43** *wit:* intellectual power.

The Reprisall

Line 6 *disentangled state:* free of debt.

Redemption

". . . the sinful state is often seen as a debtor's servitude, a state of bondage, the slavish bearing of heavy burdens, while the regenerate condition is that of release from debts and bondage and liberation from slavery" (Barbara Lewalski). See Galatians 4:1–7.

Sepulchre

Line 3 *hearts on earth:* heart = hearth. **17–20** 2 Corinthians 3:2–8.

Easter

Line 29 *We count three hundred:* the days of the year in round numbers.

Easter-wings

Line 19 *imp:* to engraft feathers in the wing of a bird, so as to repair losses or deficiencies; a term from falconry.

H. Baptisme [II]

Line 10 *Behither:* short of, barring, save.

Affliction [I]

Line 53 *crosse-bias me:* give me an inclination other than my own. A term from the game of bowls.

Prayer [I]

Line 1 *Angels age:* prayer acquaints man with the timeless existence of angels. **3** *soul in paraphrase:* in prayer the soul opens out and more fully discovers itself. **5** *Engine:* weapon; the spear that pierced Christ's side releases the blood of his reprieve and pardon. **8** *fear:* regard with reverence and awe; revere (OED, 6). **11** *Heaven in ordinarie:* a heraldic term, hence, "wearing heraldic bearings."

The H. Communion

Line 2 Joshua 7:20–21.

The Temper [I]

The title refers simultaneously to the tempering of steel, the tuning of an instrument of music and the perfecting of a human temperament. **Lines 25–28** Psalm 139:7–10.

Jordan [I]

The title asserts an equation between the holy and cleansing waters

(2 Kings 5:1–14) of Jordan and the language of piety, in specific contrast to the literary waters of Helicon and the artifices of secular poetry.

The H. Scriptures

Line 11 *Lidger:* resident ambassador. **13** *handsell:* token of good to come.

Even-song

Line 7 Psalm 130:3.

The Quidditie

Line 12 *most take all:* Hutchinson records Middleton Murry thus: "The titles to esteem which verse is not are first detailed; then it is declared that verse nevertheless is the *quiddity* of them all, in the very real sense that Herbert in his poetry comes nearest to God and most partakes of the creative power that sustains all these excellences."

Sunday

Line 27 *that is bare:* spaces between flower beds, like intervals between Sundays, are bare. **47** Judges 14:25–30.

Vertue

Line 5 *angrie:* flushed. **6** *wipe his eye:* the gazer, brought to tears by the death of the day, is roused to anger by the "military" color of the rose.

Man

Line 12 *They go upon the score:* they imitate us, read our music.

39 *distinguished:* either separated from the land as in Genesis, chapter 1, or individuated as rivers, beside which Man makes his habitation, and distinguished from waters *united* in the seas. **41** *Hath one such beautie?:* Has a single element (water) so much beauty?

Charms and Knots

Line 15 *Take one from ten:* The tithe.

Affliction [v]

Line 24 *thy bow:* both the weapon of divine wrath and the rainbow.

Mortification

Line 18 *befriend him:* the music of the church bell shall befriend man by summoning others to pray for him at the hour of his death.

Decay

Line 15 *thy thirds:* "A law-term used for the third part of a husband's estate, which went to his widow. 'Sinne' and 'Satan' have preempted the other two-thirds of the human heart" (Dudley Fitts).

The British Church

Line 5 *dates her letters:* The Church of England in Herbert's day still officially reckoned the beginning of the year from Lady Day, March 25 (the Feast of the Annunciation) and this was Herbert's practice in dating his letters.

The Quip

Line 23 *say, I am thine:* the "quip," or play on words, consists of reading this as both "Say I am thine" and "Say, 'I am thine.'" As Fitts indicates, "a paradox by punctuation."

JESU

In Herbert's day *J* and *I* were typographically the same. I-ES-U becomes "I ease you."

Dialogue

Line 4 *waving:* both wavering (i.e., vacillating) and waiving (i.e., relinquishing, surrendering).

Dulnesse

Line 19 *pretending:* both falsifying and acting as claimant (i.e., "pretender").

Sinnes round

Line 4 *cockatrice:* a fabulous creature hatched by a serpent from a cock's egg. **10** *ventilate:* to increase a flame by blowing or fanning; the cockatrice was thought to kill by its breath.

Love unknown

Line 15 *a great rock:* Exodus 17:6 and 1 Corinthians 10:4.

Paradise

"The poet lops the rhyme-words, letter by letter, much as the divine Gardener is said to *prune* and *pare*" (Hutchinson).

Artillerie

Line 17 *shooters:* shooting stars. **31** *articling:* arranging by treaty or stipulation.

The Pilgrimage

Lines 13–14 *which / Some call the wold:* a moor, an unforested, rolling plain; with a possible pun on "would." **17** *one good Angell:* a gold coin, a guardian angel and perhaps a reference to Herbert's marriage to Jane Danvers, to whom he was introduced by her kinsman Henry Danvers. **36** *a chair:* a sedan chair, a comfortable means of conveyance.

The Jews

Line 2 *cyens:* scions, slips for grafting. **5–6** Hutchinson writes: "The clue to these difficult lines must be found in St. Paul's contention that a Jew who rested in the old Law was 'a debtor to doe the whole Law' (Galatians 5:3), which was an impossible task; yet by still trying to keep the letter of the Law, instead of accepting Christ's deliverance from it (Romans 7:6), he stood to lose: *the letter* which he loses may perhaps, by a play on the word, stand also for the New Testament."

The Collar

Line 7 *thorn:* Jeremiah 12. **8–9** Either "restore with cordial fruit what I have lost," or "restore what cordial fruit has made me lose." **11** Psalm 65:9. **22** *rope of sands:* specious logic. **35** *Child:* Galatians 4:1–7.

The Pulley

Compare to the story of Pandora.

The Flower

Line 3 *demean:* bearing, demeanor; but also "demesne" or estate. **18** *a chiming:* musical, varied, as opposed to the single-toned "passing bell."

Dotage

Compare:

> *So, if I dreame I have you, I have you,*
> *For, all our joyes are but fantastical.*
> *And so I scape the paine, for paine is true;*
> *And sleepe which locks up sense, doth lock out all.*

—John Donne, "The Dreame"

Line 5 *nothing between two dishes:* A Spanish proverb.

Aaron

Exodus 28.

A Parodie

Dudley Fitts writes: "The word here has no pejorative sense. In his first two stanzas Herbert is transforming the opening of a secular poem, a love poem, into a sacred one: much as a Renaissance composer might have employed a profane melody as the *cantus* for a Mass. The original poem attributed by the best authorities to William Herbert, 3rd earl of Pembroke, begins: 'Soules joy, now I am gone,/And you alone,/(Which cannot be,/Since I must leave my selfe with thee,/And carry with me)/Yet when unto our eyes/ Absence denyes/Each others sight,/And makes to us a constant night,/When others change to light.'"

About the Editor

Anthony Hecht is currently University Professor at Georgetown University in Washington, D.C. He is the author of a number of books of poetry, including The Hard Hours, Millions of Strange Shadows *and* The Venetian Vespers. *He has also written a volume of criticism,* Obbligati: Essays in Criticism, *and is cotranslator, with Helen Bacon, of Aeschylus's* Seven Against Thebes.

The Essential Poets

Volume 1 *The Essential Keats*
Volume 2 *The Essential Whitman*
Volume 3 *The Essential Melville*
Volume 4 *The Essential Blake*
Volume 5 *The Essential Herbert*

FUTURE VOLUMES
WILL INCLUDE

The Essential Wordsworth
The Essential Campion
The Essential Hopkins
The Essential Hardy
The Essential Donne
The Essential Wyatt
The Essential Tennyson
The Essential Browning
The Essential Milton
The Essential Marvell